In the Company of Art

appearance of the galleries when installed & other
aspects of the grand renovations now underway.
Unfortunately I can see these galleries as if
I were in them, every detail. It is inimical
to sleep.

The Vincent W. Van Goghs for dinner w. the
Szarzanskis. Most gemütlich evening. Ret
roasted a leg of lamb & to it I added the
white chianti wh. was a mistake. Nevertheless
a good dinner & most convivial. Mrs. V.G. a
fun-loving soul & feels most at home in America.
They are here following Baltimore opening & en route
to N. Hampshire to visit friends. After dinner
came the Don Coxes & the Oscar Jespers, Belgian sculptor & wife. Speaking no English at
all I had an excellent opportunity to air my
French, such as it is! While Van G. is elderly
w. a lined face & white hair, his resemblance to his
uncle is very marked. Both he & his wife wear
the mantle of their distinction lightly. Both
were v. appreciative of the 'collection' chez nous,
as were the Jespers.

28 Oct.

Yesterday morning hurried to the Mus. to meet Mr &
Mrs. David Bakalar at 9:30 to show them a fine
Kokoschka & recom. the purchase of same; but
principally to ask him to buy the Erickson Rembrandt of Aristotle at the forthcoming sale for
my estimate of $1,500,000. In the spring he
told me he <u>could</u> do it. But upon pressing
131.

In the Company of Art

A Museum Director's Private Journals

PERRY T. RATHBONE

SELECTED & INTRODUCED BY

Belinda Rathbone

GODINE | BOSTON | 2024

Published in 2024 by
GODINE, PUBLISHER
Boston, Massachusetts

ENDPAPERS: Pages from the journals of Perry T. Rathbone.
COVER PHOTO: Perry Rathbone and Yousuf Karsh in the MFA's
Impressionist Gallery. Photograph © 1965 by Ivan Dmitri.
Courtesy of Belinda Rathbone.

For more information, please visit www.godine.com

LIBRARY OF CONGRESS CATALOGING-IN-PUBLICATION DATA
Names: Rathbone, Perry Townsend, 1911-2000,
author. | Rathbone, Belinda, editor.
Title: In the company of art : a museum director's private
journals / Perry T. Rathbone ; selected & introduced by Belinda
Rathbone.
Description: Boston : Godine, 2024.
Identifiers: LCCN 2023033150 (print) | LCCN 2023033151
(ebook) | ISBN 9781567928037 (hardback) |
ISBN 9781567928044 (ebook)
Subjects: LCSH: Rathbone, Perry Townsend, 1911-2000—
Diaries. | Art museum Directors—United States—Diaries.
Classification: LCC N406.R38 A3 2024 (print) |
LCC N406.R38 (ebook) | DDC 708.0092—dc23/eng/20230825
LC record available at https://lccn.loc.gov/2023033150
LC ebook record available at https://lccn.loc.gov/2023033151

First Printing, 2024
PRINTED IN THE UNITED STATES OF AMERICA

For Peter and Eliza

CONTENTS

INTRODUCTION

For much of his thirty-two-year career as a museum director, my father kept a private journal. When the mood struck and time allowed, alone in his study at the end of an evening, perhaps a nightcap in hand, he penned his entries in a large, unlined sketchbook. He wrote of the pleasures and the woes of his work at the museum, and the ambiance of many a dinner party. He also wrote intimately of his domestic and family life. To read his journal years later, full of names overheard in the conversational banter that had floated around our house, was to reimagine those times as he lived them and to know him in a new way. Whereas my mother's leatherbound pocket diaries record the facts of our family life, my father's journals are filled with his feelings.

The greatest concentration of his journal writing is from the early 1960s, during his directorship of the Museum of Fine Arts (MFA) in Boston. These were exciting times, as he began to enjoy the rewards of his achievements since his arrival at the museum in 1955. Coming from his successful fifteen-year directorship at the moderately sized St. Louis Art Museum, he had faced what he called a slumbering giant of a museum in Boston, which had been his challenge to awaken. As the MFA's dynamic and popular new director, he cut a prominent figure in Boston society, and as a cultural leader his attention and opinion were widely sought. In his early fifties he was at the peak of his powers, at the crest of his career, old enough to look back as far as he could look forward. It was at this point of reckoning that he took up journal writing in earnest.

Why did he write? Who was it for? "Is it a waste?" he asked himself in October 1962, and then answered, "In looking back over the preceding pages, I know how omnivorous time swallows up the detail of our lives. I am astonished at how much of this trivia I would have totally forgotten had I not written it down." He wrote, in other words, for his own sake—to remember what he had seen and whom he had met, to unload his hopes and anxieties onto paper, to exult in his joys. I suspect that he also wrote out of an interest in exercising his skills as a diarist. And while the entries are clearly not written for publication as is, there are signs that he wrote with an idea that they might someday be of value to others. "Again David Pickman [former head of public relations at the MFA] *urged* me to make notes about my life," he wrote in May 1973, "that guarantees at least one reader!" That entry—among his last—seems to provide adequate grounds for sharing this buried treasure some fifty years on. With the consent of my brother, Peter, and sister, Eliza, and their invaluable collaboration in editing the journals, I offer to the reader what is perhaps even more interesting and certainly less guarded than the memoirs our father never wrote.

PERRY RATHBONE (1911–2000) was among the first generation of trained museum professionals who shaped a modern era of American art museums in the mid-twentieth century. This was largely thanks to a post-graduate course at Harvard called Museum Work and Museum Problems, which was conceived and taught by Paul Sachs beginning in 1921, and in which Rathbone enrolled after earning his undergraduate degree in art history in 1933. The course created a standard of professionalism and a network amongst its graduates, whose collective influence was inestimable. Throughout his career, Rathbone collaborated with fellow museum directors and curators for exhibitions and loans and competed with them for patrons and collections. A fraternity of rivals, together they steered American art museums through times of enormous growth as the postwar era demanded a wholesale reimagining of the staid Victorian mausoleums of their grandparents' day.

As director of the St. Louis Art Museum from 1940 to 1955 and the Museum of Fine Arts in Boston from 1955 to 1972, Rathbone vastly increased membership and attendance, programs and publications. He renovated galleries and facilities, introduced modern and contemporary art, and ushered these museums into the modern era with more than a touch of class. But he often quoted Paul Sachs' sage reminder, "A museum man's name is written in sand." Knowing how easily his achievements would be forgotten or eclipsed by subsequent generations, he took the greatest pride in his acquisitions of timeless masterpieces for his museums' permanent collections.

As part of the training of the museum course, students were taught by Sachs' example and as guests at his dinner table how to entertain trustees, collectors, and visiting dignitaries from around the world. No one took this aspect of the museum director's role more seriously and with more gusto than Perry Rathbone. In the pages of his journal, Aldous Huxley, Sir Kenneth Clark, and Prince Umberto of Italy are among the notables who were given private tours of the MFA, all in the interest of spreading the word of Boston's great museum. Endowed by nature with a buoyant manner of optimism and warmth, he sought to make every business encounter personal. As much as possible he entertained at our home on Coolidge Hill in Cambridge, where my mother, Euretta de Cosson Rathbone, regularly rose to the challenge, often receiving out-of-town guests and complete strangers for dinner at a moment's notice. Before every important exhibition opening at the museum, they hosted a dinner party for lenders and VIPs. As children we learned to anticipate the arrival of the help in our kitchen, and later the sounds of animated greetings in the front hall as the dinner guests arrived with the rustle of evening dresses, a blend of expensive perfume wafting up the stairs. On these occasions my father enjoyed showing off his collection of modern art acquired on his modest budget in the 1940s as well as setting the table with heirlooms from both sides of our family. These were the pleasures of entertaining at home.

Equally, as a guest he never took another's domestic environment for granted. Every house or apartment he entered he sized up, for it told volumes about its owners' history; there was always something to learn about and possibly to solicit as a gift for the museum. The journals are full of his appreciation for the old-fashioned style of Boston interiors of the day, and especially how Bostonians "have a way of accepting what already exists." At Mrs. Bayard Warren's house on the North Shore, he admired "her big paneled and tapestried house; dark and rich and lofty rooms with immense fireplaces in the high taste of fifty years ago."

He was almost as comfortable among the Boston Brahmins with generations of familial ties to the MFA—the Lowells, the Lambs, the Coolidges, and the Codmans, to name a few—as he was among the artists and intellectuals of Cambridge. In this sense he hovered somewhere mid-Charles River, between die-hard traditional values and liberal nonconformity, between black tie men's club dinners in Boston and crowded Cambridge cocktail parties. Unlike many residents of one or the other city, he crossed that bridge virtually every day, from his home to his office and back again.

This ease of transition was due to his natural sympathy for both camps while not being strictly a member of either one. Growing up in New York City and upstate, he was not a Brahmin, although he had Puritan roots just as deep; nor was he an academic, but more a generalist of many enthusiasms. Trained in the courtship of the rich, he also learned to see through them. "Like so many of the rich I have known," he wrote of New York socialite C. Z. Guest in 1963, "she seems almost to hate it," while G. David Thompson, the Philadelphia millionaire, "has graduated from being an eccentric art collector to simply 'keeping up with the Rockefellers.'" He wrote candidly of the collectors and patrons he cultivated, entertained, and forbore, sometimes confiding to his journal an impatience he would never have shown them in person. After a meeting with American art collector Maxim Karolik, he wrote, "The harangue required that we listen to the entire history of the formation of the collection, a story I have heard at least a hundred times in five years." He was occasionally dismayed at the ignorance of his trustees when presenting a work of art for their approval. At a lukewarm reception of a painting by Whistler, he summed up one trustee as "an admirable man of the law but possessing not a fiber of aesthetic sensibility."

His own was forever stimulated by the works of art around him, whether the latest object of his desire on display in his office or a masterwork freshly restored to its original glow in the conservation lab. "From under an old veil of discolored varnish and dirt," he writes of *Carriage at the Races*—a small oil by Degas—"emerges a landscape with figures bathed in clean air, a sky dotted with tiny puffs of vapor."

In the early 1960s, Boston's skyline was rapidly changing. When the fifty-two-story Prudential Tower rose incongruously in the heart of the Back Bay in 1964, it was a shock to the cityscape of Victorian townhouses, virtually undisturbed since their construction nearly one hundred years earlier. Around the same time, a cluster of skyscrapers sprouted along the narrow, crooked streets of downtown Boston. In Cambridge, meanwhile, Josep Lluís Sert, then head of the Harvard Graduate School of Design, seeded his modernist influence on the cityscape with buildings such as Holyoke Center in Harvard Square and Le Corbusier's only building in America, the Carpenter Center for the Visual Arts. My father deplored "the monstrous new building . . . that destroys the unity of Quincy St., having no relationship whatsoever to its surroundings," and in general Harvard's self-interested grip over zoning laws in Cambridge. Especially because at the same time, his alma mater was neglecting its own historic monuments such as Memorial Hall, which lost its clock tower to a fire in 1956, and Elmwood, now the official residence of the president of Harvard, which in the mid-1960s had "all the personality of a hotel room."

For as much as he could be a powerful activist for change, at his core Rathbone was a passionate preservationist—an advocate for history, beauty, visual coherence, and authenticity—in the sense that a museum director must be. As an art czar and an arbiter of taste, he aired his views about the urban landscape fervently and often publicly. He was on the front lines of the battle against the "Inner Belt" when it threatened to tear an interstate highway through Boston and Cambridge in the early 1960s, and the widening of the sycamore-lined Memorial

Drive along the Charles River. "Americans in the middle of the twentieth century live at the mercy of highway engineers and 'traffic experts,'" he despaired in 1964.

The years he covered most thoroughly in his journals were those of the Kennedy White House, and he was excited to align himself with their youth, optimism, and high cultural aspirations, especially with the preservationist zeal of Jacqueline Kennedy. But he also felt his age in his first meeting with her at the White House in 1961. "Her ultra-simple attire made me feel that I belonged to a different generation . . . a starkly simple dark blue dress, bare arms, no stockings, simple black low heeled shoes, no jewelry," he observed in April 1961. Indeed it was a time when his own children were entering their teen years, when the last of the Victorians were face-to-face with adolescent baby boomers in bellbottom blue jeans and miniskirts. While he would gamely join a pulsing dance floor of teenagers doing the twist, there was nothing he enjoyed more than a reason for donning his white tie and tails. He found himself at the crossroads of the generation gap, adjusting his eyes to the view. After a private dance at the Ritz in Boston, he wrote, "Somehow these debutante parties lack the glamour, the 'occasion,' that they certainly possessed when I was a youth. I suppose the basic reason is that their social meaning is dwindling."

The art world, meanwhile, was convulsing in a spectrum of new directions in the 1960s, while my father was struggling to build a collection of modern art for a museum that had barely broken into the twentieth century when he arrived in 1955 and was by that time far behind. The price of mid-century moderns was rising, while the supply of old masters dwindled. His journal records the excitement in the room "replete with all the greats of the country's art world," at the record-breaking sale of

Rembrandt's *Aristotle* at Parke-Bernet in 1961. Keeping up with the competition meant regular trips to New York to visit "more and more dealers to see fewer and fewer desirable pictures," and a sojourn of several weeks in Europe every summer, where his hectic itinerary jetting between art capitals combined business with pleasure. While traveling, he wrote letters home to my mother on tissue-thin air stationary that help to fill in where the journals leave off in his absences from Cambridge—tales of his visits to Picasso in the South of France, Peggy Guggenheim in Venice, and Henry McIlhenny in Donegal.

My father's journal writing trailed off in the later 1960s, when his workload became ever more demanding as the MFA approached its centennial year: 1970. "Months of neglect stare me in the face," he apologized to his journal in September 1965. As someone once warned him, a centennial is a fate worse than death, and he was to understand that admonition fully by the time he retired from the MFA in 1972. The decisive moment of his ill-fated acquisition of the small Italian painting that ultimately led to his resignation is documented here in his letter to my mother of July 15, 1969. The consequences of that moment—his acquisition for the MFA of the so-called "Boston Raphael,"—are well documented in oral histories, innumerable press stories, and his own white paper. But the innocence and excitement he expresses in this private missive is all we have about his state of mind at the time, and is all the more touching in retrospect. It was a pivotal event that signaled the beginning of an era of repatriation, controversies over which continue to roil the art world to this day.

The journal therefore leads up to a critical turning point, full of my father's natural optimism along with a new kind of anxiety about "an age of discontinuity and change" where he now found himself. We read in real time of the Cuban Missile Crisis, Kennedy's assassination, John Glenn's first orbit of the globe, racial unrest, and the Vietnam War. All along, the role of the museum director was evolving in ways the museum course at Harvard could not have prepared him for. But his abiding belief in the power of art to enhance the lives of his public was never diminished, nor—as his journals attest—was his love of life.

—BELINDA RATHBONE

ST. LOUIS

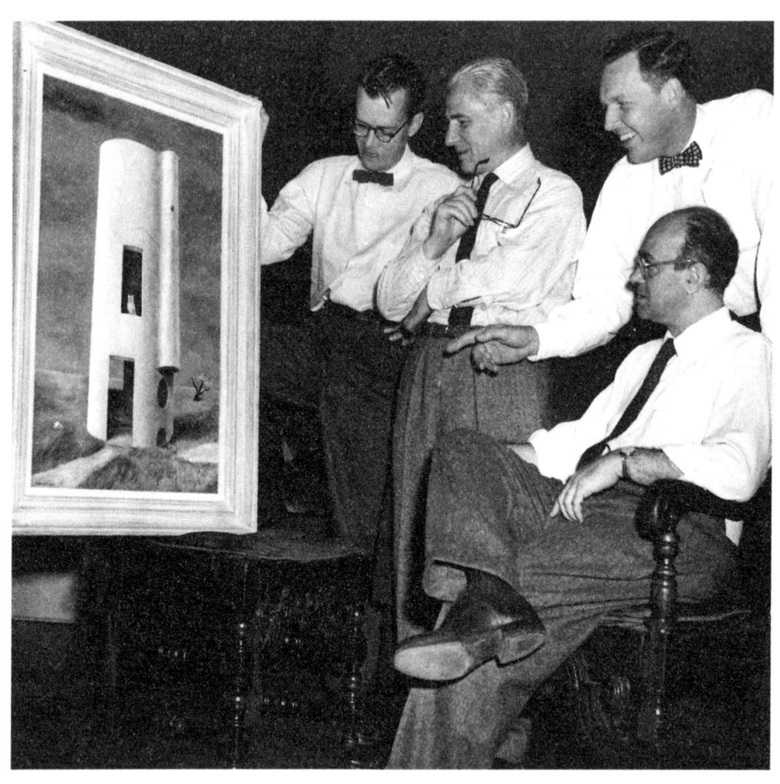

Perry Rathbone (third from left) and Willem de Kooning (second from left) jurying an art show at the Chicago Art Institute in 1953.

In Chicago last week judging the Chicago Annual at the Art Institute.[1] There met Willem de Kooning, co-juror. After giving him the benefit of the doubt for two days, decided he was a man of limited intelligence. Nice enough and agreeable, but he made no remarks that revealed particular insights. All this surprised me as I thought I had detected a trace of poetry in his work. Has eyes like a doll, blue and staring. Quite expressionless. And a staccato monotony of speech I found rather tiring.

Dined at the Walter Andersons' and got a penthouse view of Chicago by night with the Wrigley Building like an incandescent torch in the midst of it. Very beautiful and strange, but somehow not to be loved. Too bad [Paul] Klee never saw a skyscraper city at night. He would have caught and distilled the magic. Only [Lyonel] Feininger and [William] Congdon (ones that I know of) have conveyed this in the mid-century. Franklin Boggs from Beloit also co-juror and also chez Anderson. A nice, boyish American. Bluff and enthusiastic. A man of good taste and now an associate of my sculptor friend Clark Fitz-Gerald at the Wisconsin College.

After went to the [Jay Z. and Muriel] Steinbergs' apt, miles up the shore. Place filled with avant-garde this and that: some hideous muck by [Jean] Dubuffet, a pathetic [Philip] Guston

---

1. Rathbone was frequently called upon as a juror or judge for art exhibitions and contests and enjoyed the exercise and the camaraderie of fellow jurors.

and a large group of (to me) little-knowns. Things by [Franz] Kline in black and white paint (therefore paintings) that ought at best to be confined to the pages of a sketchbook. But a good lyric [Joan] Miró and a handsome [Nicolas] de Staël. And a de Kooning of course. This decorative panel de K. states was inspired by a sink in his studio. Started with that in the lower center and after that he said he didn't know what he was doing. Everyone else thought they saw exotic symbols in it.

No, said de K.

In two days we looked at sixteen hundred pictures. It gave me an uncontrollable desire to look at just one good work of art which I did as soon as possible.

5 OCTOBER 1953

When I was in N.Y. last month Curt Valentin[2] was closing his books. He told me he had done $454,000 worth of business in the preceding twelve months. His first year in N.Y., 1937–38, he did $15,000 worth and thought that good. Dr. Johnson said a man should take pains to keep his friendships in good repair. No one understands that precept better than C. V. He never permits one to forget him. From numerous little attentions he is not long absent from one's thoughts. He never buys one catalogue, but a dozen and distributes them liberally amongst his friends. He is even more generous with his own publications

---

2. Curt Valentin (1902–1954) arrived as a refugee from Nazi Germany in 1937 to run the Buchholz Gallery (later the Curt Valentin Gallery from 1951–1955) in midtown Manhattan. A champion of art branded "degenerate" by the Nazis, he was a leading purveyor of European modernism to American museums and private collectors and was highly influential in shaping Rathbone's eye and taste early in his career. Valentin died of a heart attack while visiting Marino Marini in Forte dei Marmi in 1954.

which are numerous and always excellent. No dealer has contributed so much to contemporary art literature. This bolsters his reputation as a serious and sincere lover of art and together with his honesty, integrity, his unfailing good taste and his harmonious relations with artists, accounts for his phenomenal success.

He has created a new taste and enthusiasm for sculpture which has an especial appeal for his sensuous nature. Most dealers are too lazy to handle sculpture. Not Valentin. He once told me that if his 57th St competition knew how much he made handling sculpture they'd faint.

14 OCTOBER 1953

Hanging the Van Gogh show. A tiring job and a difficult one. But just to be with those pictures is such a joy!

It is now just a year since Mrs. Mark Steinberg[3] bought her first picture, the Degas pastel of two dancers—and fell in love with it. And then with the idea of having a collection. The picture brought life and character to her house which, for all its tasteful beauty it had lacked. Mrs. S. had the eyes and the intelligence to recognize it. Almost at once she wanted more of the same. Unlike many new collectors, she decided from the start that only the best would do. And her natural liberality easily permitted her to make this decision. The Degas came from Knoedler's and cost $28,000.

In January we met in New York with her daughter and

---

3. Etta (Mrs. Mark) Steinberg, then recently widowed and in charge of a considerable charitable trust, became an important patron of the St. Louis Art Museum, collecting impressionist and post-impressionist paintings with the intention of donating the works to the museum. She was closely advised by Rathbone.

son-in-law.[4] For three days we made the rounds of the galleries visiting eleven dealers looking at dozens of impressionist and post-impressionist paintings—all winners, at a cost of $148,000. They were a Van Gogh, a Renoir, a Manet, a Pissarro and a Fantin-Latour. The Van Gogh is a large view of Auvers, a harmony of blue and green with deep receding space, a joyous picture full of light and air. This from Paul Rosenberg who I induced to knock $5,000 off his asking price. Formerly it had belonged to Captain Molyneux and before that to Hugo von Tschudi.[5] R[osenberg] had already sold so much in his fiscal year that he refused to be paid until after Sept. 1. The Renoir is of Mme Massonie, a commissioned portrait of about 1870. A painting of sumptuous richness in color, texture and form. A deep blue gown, crimson roses, blond hair, touches of gold and moiré background. The type is odd, unbeautiful but sensitive and very affecting. It is virtually an unknown picture having come directly from the family. I think it a great Renoir. When [William] Davidson[6] quoted $35,000 I was amazed and more amazed when he accepted $28,000.

18 OCTOBER 1953

Mrs. Steinberg's Manet, *Chanteuse de Café-Concert* is a radiant picture and a dazzling performance technically. Painted alla prima in tones of blue, pink, and white it has a fragrance and

---

4. Richard "Dick" and Florence Weil.

5. Hugo von Tschudi (1851–1911) was director of the Berlin National Gallery from 1896–1909 and an avid collector of impressionist and post-impressionist works of art.

6. William Davidson was with Knoedler Gallery in New York from 1920–1971.

charm combined with strength that is peculiarly French. This was a [Auguste] Pellerin picture and came from [Sam] Salz who had brought it over from Reid and Lefèvre. S. asked $46,000 and finally settled for $35,000. Dick Weil left the bargaining to me and for the first and only time in my experience a dealer attempted to proposition me. The painting was apparently on consignment to Salz and he proposed that the price be fixed at $40,000 and that we divide $5,000 between us! I was scandalized. The very thought made me frightfully uncomfortable. But without losing my temper or creating a scene, knowing how easily this weasel takes offence, I simply told him he was talking to the wrong man. Then he tried to give me a drawing. And when I also rejected that idea, he told me to forget about it. But I couldn't. It weighed on my mind and I told the whole ugly story to Dick Weil at the first opportunity. Salz is a repellant creature, but he cannot be ignored.

7 FEBRUARY 1954

David Röell[7] dined here last night. Only Martha [Love][8] with us and a very congenial company. Röell is a sociable sort with a sound appetite for conversation. He relished food and drink and tobacco like a good Dutchman. He is modest and slightly shy, but self-possessed. His taste is impeccable, his connoisseurship highly regarded both sides of the Atlantic. His appetite for looking at works of art is like his appetite for conversation and

---

7. David Röell (1894–1961) was director of the Rijksmuseum from 1945–1959.
8. Martha Love (1907–1993), a close family friend who was responsible for introducing Perry to Rettles Rathbone in 1940, was a patron of the St. Louis Art Museum and its first woman trustee.

the other quiet amenities of life—practically inexhaustible. I was more pleased to see him than any European colleague at the Metropolitan congress in N.Y. That he should want to visit St. Louis after an interval of eight years I accept as a profound compliment. Many new acquisitions interested him, as well as old ones. In praise of the Zurbarán still life he could not say enough. That he much preferred it to the Contini[9] version in spite of the signature on the latter meant more to me than all the comments and critical opinion it has provoked. He remembered the Contini one in the Paris still life show and found it wanting in color and subtlety of design compared with ours.

I made the usual round of collections with him—Steinbergs, [Robert H.] Shoenbergs,[10] [Joseph] Pulitzers.[11] Of the Steinberg paintings his choice was 1) Van Gogh 2) Lautrec 3) Renoir. The Shoenberg Manet, Pissarro and Monet satisfied him most. He explored the Pulitzer collection with Joe and extolled the Ingres drawing, finding it superior to the *Duke of Bedford* at the museum which he had already greatly admired.

Röell by way of gossip told us that Jacques Dupont and Germain Bazin were rivals for Georges Salles' post at the Louvre and that they cordially disliked one another.

---

9. Count Alessandro Contini-Bonacossi (1878–1955) was an Italian politician and art collector.

10. Robert and Jean Shoenberg were collectors of modern art and important philanthropists to St. Louis institutions.

11. Joseph "Joe" Pulitzer Jr. (1913–1993), third in his family line as editor of the *St. Louis Post-Dispatch*, and his wife Louise "Lulu" Vauclain Pulitzer (1914–1968) were leading collectors of modern art in St. Louis, setting an example by collecting daringly in the art of their time. Pulitzer was an enormously supportive friend to Rathbone at the museum and in the press.

Bazin and wife were here 1 Feb. He lectured on the last days of Van Gogh having been represented to me by Frankfurter as capable of doing a lecture in English or French. For us he spoke "English" which no one understood. But this did not phase the redoubtable and self-important Bazin. He forced us all to speak French the two days he was here. But he was immensely interesting in discussing the São Paulo Museum and the amazing Chateaubriand, the exhibition in Paris, etc. Also v. interesting on the subject of French painters today. Virtually all of them except [Georges] Rouault are communists or left-wingers. Even Matisse, the darling of American capitalists.

Bazin also greatly admired the Zurbarán still life and surprised me by showing such enthusiasm for Max Beckmann. The paintings at home as well as those in the Pulitzer collection impressed him deeply: their strength and richness of *matière* he commented upon. He liked the *Baou de Saint-Jeannet* and Rettles' portrait[12] best. Röell also admired the latter and the still life considering it one of the very best of the Amsterdam period.

At Joe [Pulitzer]'s, Bazin observed that as an American he had characteristically chosen the best examples of twentieth century French painters—the significant, forceful pictures. Such paintings one does not find in French collections, the French preferring the "safe" more traditional and less vigorous expressions.

---

12. Max Beckmann's portrait of Rettles Rathbone was the first portrait he painted after arriving in America in 1947. It is now in the collection of the Museum of Fine Arts, Boston, along with Beckmann's 1948 portrait of Perry T. Rathbone.

BOSTON

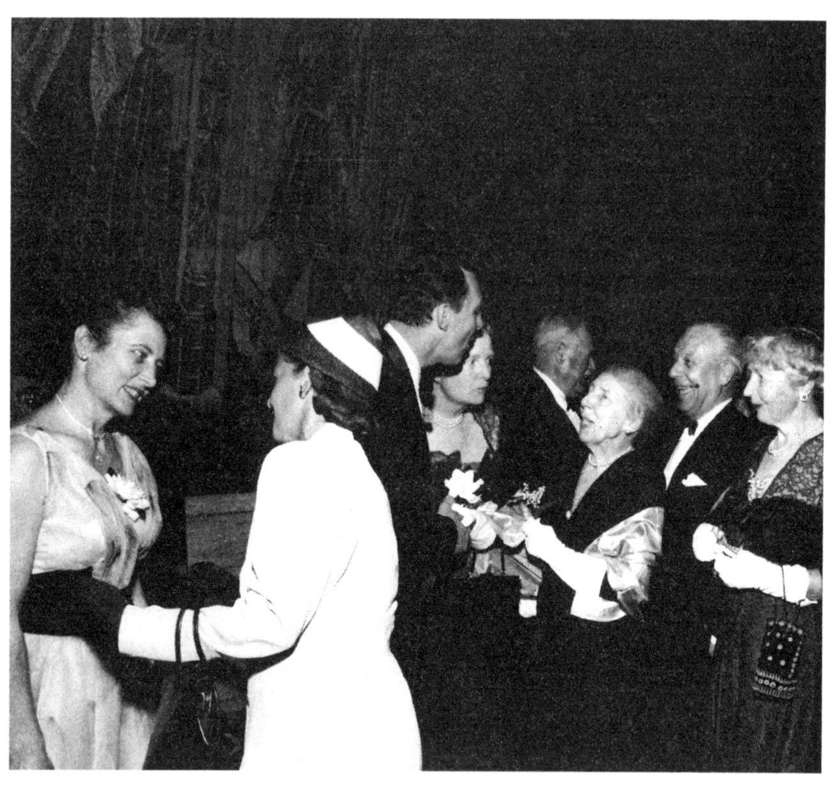

*Mr. and Mrs. Perry Rathbone meet the Boston Brahmins
in a receiving line at the MFA in May 1955.*

Darling Ret,[1]

I have looked at ten houses for sale and one to rent. Only one would you be happy to buy, I'm sure, and that's the Rockwoods', Coolidge Hill.[2] The rental (July 1st–Feb 1st) you would also like. It's on Coolidge Hill, cheerful and big enough. $250 and I suppose we have to heat it ourselves. If I should land you in some of the others, the whole family would break into tears on sight!

I looked at another this noon. Nice street (Elmwood Ave.) near schools, size about right, price possible ($37,000); but frame, about 1890, kitchen and bathrooms rather terrible, dining room and study too small and unattractive, no hall closet, yard impoverished—a house of no distinction. Just house. Drawing room rather good, about size of Windermere. It would take $10,000 to make it anything we would like, and we'd be torn up how long? So, I'm discouraged again.

Looked at Shady Hill[3] again, just for fun. It's certainly big,

---

1. Rathbone's wife, Euretta de Cosson Rathbone (1909–2003), was called Rettles, or Ret (or Rett).

2. 151 Coolidge Hill, a spacious brick colonial with a large garden, was the house the Rathbones bought in 1955 and was their home for the next thirty years.

3. Shady Hill, an 1806 mansion house in Cambridge, was owned by a succession of Harvard professors. Paul Sachs occupied Shady Hill while a professor of fine arts at Harvard and held classes there for his museum course students. In the 1950s the house was up for sale, and

but pretty. The Sachses urged me to look into it again. And maybe I will, but I'm not at all hopeful. Perhaps I will have to go to Brookline where I'm told there's something very good for 25. But that means changing schools and making new friends.

Everyone seems to think you should come for the shindig the 24th. Museum would pay expenses. I know you hate to do it and I hate to ask you, but if you can, please come. It would also help to decide this awful house problem and you should plan to be here two days.

I find there is almost nothing about the Boston Museum[4] that is attractive except the staff and the collections and the members of the Board I have met. To think of overhauling it really tries my faith and courage. What dreary galleries, what gloom! And what a behemoth it is! Everybody here is encouraging and it's a good thing too! Paul Sachs is magnificent that way. No man could have a better booster or more loyal backer. The trouble is I still feel alone and up to my ears in an avalanche of problems.

The staff is very easy going. They all go home at 4:30! No Saturdays. The other day at five o'clock I wondered where everybody was!

I have a new secretary who is pregnant and isn't going to stay. Not much good anyway. Tomorrow—Saturday—I have three prospects coming in. Also a girl from a Wellesley College paper to interview me. Monday I have a half hour

---

Rathbone, with fond memories of his student days, was interested but ultimately thought better of it. The house was soon afterward demolished to make room for a new building for the American Academy of Arts and Sciences.

4. Rathbone was appointed director of the Museum of Fine Arts in Boston in 1955. He made several trips to Boston from St. Louis during this transitional period.

television interview at 6:30. Then Committee, School and Board meetings next week, a whole gang of them.

I dined with the Sachses alone on Wednesday, and had a wonderful long talk with Paul[5] until midnight. He says it will take me five years to get on top of the job! But I feel I have been two months already!

In my wildest dreams I never thought I would be inhabiting this palace.[6] It is very odd. My room is a block away from the living room and because the house is built around a court, you have to go round the block to get there! The Stouts struggle valiantly with Mrs. Gardner's old and ornery furniture, trying to create a home here and still not offend the erstwhile tenant, Morris Carter who thinks nothing should be touched.[7]

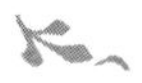

HOTEL BAYERISCHER HOF MÜNCHEN, MUNICH, GERMANY, 15 SEPTEMBER 1956 (ABOARD AIR FRANCE TO PARIS)

To continue, Darling,

I was abruptly interrupted and had to address, seal, and stamp envelope. So I was last aboard the plane.

Peggy Guggenheim is a nice—very nice, straightforward,

---

5. Paul Sachs (1878–1965) taught the legendary museum course at Harvard's Fogg Art Museum from 1921–1948, training a generation of museum professionals. Rathbone was a member of one of his largest classes in 1933–'34 and was among his most notable graduates.
6. Rathbone was the guest of George Stout (1897–1978), director of the Isabella Stewart Gardner Museum (Fenway Court) from 1955–1970, and his wife Margie on many of his introductory visits to the MFA.
7. Mrs. Gardner instructed in her will that the curator of her museum reside as she had in the private fourth floor living quarters of the palace. This was discontinued in 1990.

plain speaking neurotic creature living in simple luxury in a half-ruin on the Grand Canal.[8] Hospitality is not one of her failings. She seemed to take a liking to me after the first drink and was horrified by the idea of my spending a minute in the San Marco. Before I knew it I was part of the household—here in that house that had rather chilled me when I visited it in her absence two years ago. Peggy lives amidst the considerable confusion of nine Lhasa terriers—little bundles of wool with cute faces, and the constant ebb and flow of visitors. These consist of the international art-literary set and the diplomatic. Not the social, least of all that of Venice which is ultra-aloof. But there wouldn't be room for these people anyway.

Somebody comes for drinks every day and one day there was a party for thirty-odd—amongst them were Mary McCarthy (of Venice articles in *New Yorker*) and her willowy husband, Broadwater, who teaches Latin at St. Bernard's, New York; Virgil Thomson, Graham and Catherine Sutherland, Oliver Wessel, Arthur Jeffress, Lady Oonagh something-or-other, who was a Guinness, Peggy's daughter, Pegeen Hélion etc etc. In this atmosphere *exotique* I lived for three days. I exhausted myself at the Biennale which I thought indescribably bad and it is unbelievably big. Then the Delacroix show and in between times numerous churches with altarpieces and ceilings and always endless walking until I got a blister in my toe. Alessandro Brass invited me to lunch and Peggy had me delivered there in a gondola. I really felt like the Prince of [illegible] floating down the Grand Canal in this sleek craft shining like patent leather, her liveried gondolier

---

8. Peggy Guggenheim (1898–1979) bought the Palazzo Venier dei Leoni in Venice in the late 1940s and filled it with her ever-growing collection of modern art. After his initial visit in 1956, at Guggenheim's urging, Rathbone made a habit of spending a few days as her houseguest on his summer sojourns through Europe.

behind me. But I felt terribly solo and a little ridiculous. *You* should have been with me. Brass had nothing too exciting to see, but the lunch was good. Peggy Guggenheim is giving the museum an [Jean] Hélion (he is her son-in-law) and I am going to his studio today to select it. She also would entertain the idea of leaving her whole modern art collection to Boston. Alfred Barr and Jim Sweeney have courted her vigorously, but she's interested in Boston's need.[9] So, my time was not wasted. Her gondolier took me to the airlines office in her motor launch Thursday am, then a long bus ride to Treviso for the plane.

HOTEL AM ZOO, BERLIN, 1957

Dearest Wife,

The weekend in Hamburg was really like a holiday and that is what [Alfred] Hentzen[10] and [Erich] Meyer[11] wanted. We needed it for while travelling and looking is fun, it is also hard work. And Hamburg was refreshing too because the destruction there is much less obvious—the museums practically intact (unfortunately!); even the famous railway station appears undamaged and for the first time we stopped at an old hotel with high ceilings and room to swing a cat.

---

9. Rathbone actively courted Guggenheim in the interest of building up the MFA's modern art holdings, but in the end she bequeathed most of her collection to her Uncle Solomon's Guggenheim Museum in New York.

10. Alfred Hentzen (1903–1985) was director of the Hamburger Kunsthalle.

11. Erich Meyer (1897–1967) was an art historian. In 1957 Alfred Hentzen was working on the Festschrift for Meyer's sixtieth birthday, which was published by Hauswedell.

There were luncheons, cocktail and coffee parties, visits to dealers as well as museums and all amidst beautiful weather and the exceptionally pretty outskirts of the city with waterways full of boats and always an intriguing reminiscence of England about the scene.

Alf and Meyer gave a big cocktail party at the Hentzens' apartment which led to a wild evening at St. Pauli, the famous honky-tonk quarter of the port. We drank beer and danced at the Saverin Zillerthal where Perry Cott[12] led the band in the "Stars and Stripes Forever" and we all danced on the tables. Finally we all landed in a tiny underground boîte called Barcelona where all the "girls" turned out to be men— really unbelievable, especially an old Spanish "signorita." The dealer [Ernst] Hauswedell was the *gruppenführer* of this crawl which ended in a café at 5 am where we had delicious Milnerbruehe and called it a night. Next day (Sunday) the Meyers entertained us all at buffet lunch at their house and garden in the outskirts which was enchanting, lovely weather, delicious food and wine and the nicest people, the Meyers pretty house is a modest one but it contains a library of eight thousand volumes! The M.'s were so happy to know you and the children and constantly referred to the pleasures of Cambridge and can't wait to return. And you would love Anne Hentzen—one of the best museum wives.

So we sadly bid farewell to Hamburg Monday noon having spent the morning at Alf [Hentzen]'s museum. We flew BEA to Berlin in a new English turbo-prop plane—the smoothest landing and takeoff I can remember and relatively quiet. Here we are in the midst of fantastic destruction again, great fields of weeds and cragged ruins. But on the other hand the shell-

---

12. Perry Cott (1909–1998) was chief curator at the National Gallery of Art, Washington, DC.

torn stump of the old Kaiser Wilhelm Gedächtnis Kirche commands the Kurfürstendamm which is largely rebuilt and as lively and brightly lit as the Hollywood strip.

This morning we went on an exhausting three and a half hour bus tour of all of West Berlin accompanied by a number of the city plan board explaining everything from rubble disposal to the new highway system; we visited an old people's home and climbed on the tumbled remains of the Wilhelmstrasse. Then we collapsed for lunch in Dahlem near the Gemäldegalerie which we afterwards visited to see the Kaiser Friedrich pictures and to see [Friedrich] Winkler.

I am impressed with the enterprise and liveliness of Berlin West, by the seeming prosperity and normality of the place as it rises from the incredible ruins. And I suppose that is what the Germans want us to see and to feel—hence our no less than six days here.

16 MAY 1958

"Harvard is a seminary for discussion as well as for conviction." This was the reply of Samuel Willard[13] to one Keith, a Quaker who came to Cambridge to question Willard's theology. It is probably one of the first expressions of Harvard's policy of academic freedom. This bit was communicated to

---

13. Samuel Willard was Rathbone's direct ancestor, a second-generation Bostonian from Kent, England, who was minister of Old South Church and acting president of Harvard College from 1701 to 1707. He was remembered for his courageous defense of a woman on trial for witchcraft. Rathbone was exceedingly proud of his Willard ancestry.

me by Dick Gummere, member of The Club,[14] former dean of admissions at Harvard, and historian. Strange satisfaction in having one's ancestor discussed as an historical and intellectual personage.

It was a meeting of The Club at William T. Aldrich's[15] house in Brookline. Those present round the well butlered table and in the pleasant French drawing room were beside our host, his brother Winthrop, recently ambassador to the court of St. James, Paul Sachs, Clarence Haring, Walter D. Edmonds, Richard Gummere, Mark Howe, W[illia]m. James, and Walter Whitehill as guest. Billy Aldrich was immensely entertaining recounting his personal history from the age of three through his student days at the Beaux Arts. He's a gay and humorous man at seventy-eight and extraordinarily tolerant of modern architectural developments considering his training. Am always surprised and impressed at how human and natural the rich and famous *can* be. Aldrich is one of them.

Architects never have any real appreciation of the other plastic arts. W. T. Aldrich no exception. In all that big house and after years of education and travel and ample means, the pictures are inconsequential. There is no sculpture.

---

14. The Club was one of several men's clubs Rathbone belonged to in Boston, in this case without a dedicated clubhouse, so that members met in other clubs or at each other's homes for dinner and a lecture by the hosting member. Rathbone was also a member of the Somerset Club, the Tavern Club, the Harvard Club, and the Club of Odd Volumes.

15. William T. Aldrich (1880–1966) was a neoclassical architect of residential and museum buildings, including the Worcester Art Museum and the Rhode Island School of Design Museum.

14 MARCH 1959

A brilliant dinner at the Signet Society with John Finley[16] of Harvard faculty as toastmaster, Phil Hofer retiring president, Nate Pusey, Mac Bundy, Walter D. Edmonds the new president, Ed Streeter, author of *Dear Mabel*—who received the Signet medal for contribution to the arts. Toby Sizer of Yale representing the Elizabethan Society whose seventy-fifth anniversary was celebrated, the poet [Richard] Wilbur who collaborated on musical of *Candide* and not least August Heckscher[17] who spoke brilliantly on the crowding of the world in "the age of space" likening ourselves and our world to those who must have felt darkness in the Age of Enlightenment. He spoke of values being lost in the dissolution of the city—values that could only arise and find cultivation thanks to density and population and intimate communication resulting therefore. He spoke with alarm at the forty-seven million additional human beings born into the world each year. He spoke of disappearing entities such as clean-cut nations on the map owing to overlapping. He spoke of a million acres a year that are sacrificed to expanding urban development—tilled land, wild land given over to macadam, concrete ribbons and seas of asphalt.

Heckscher spoke resting his little page of notes on top of a candlestick. He spoke fluently and with phrasing worthy of the most cultivated Englishman. In deference to Elizabeth (I) he

---

16. John Finley (1904–1995) was a classics professor at Harvard and master of Eliot House from 1941 to 1968.
17. August "Augie" Heckscher (1913–1997) was a well-known lecturer on politics and the arts. He was an adviser to the Kennedy administration on cultural matters and New York City parks commissioner from 1967 to 1972.

told story of a magnificent masque which she and her courtiers attended. At close, Leicester, or one of them asked her majesty if they would dance at which she exclaimed "What! After such a banquet, bread and cheese!" Heckscher modestly referred to his "remarks" as bread and cheese following as it did the reading of four poems by Wilbur and Streeter's speech of acceptance, not to mention the witty, sparkling and humane performance of John Finley as well.

It was perhaps the most civilized evening I have spent in Cambridge. And it seemed to be the general agreement that it was an exceptional night, even for the Signet. Heckscher led off by referring nostalgically to "the expansive age of Elizabeth" then developed his thesis of how cramped we are in the age of space both physically and spiritually. He spoke of modern houses that are described as "giving the illusion of space." The real thing is denied us.

14 JULY 1959

This afternoon Ret and I to J[osep] L[luís] Sert's[18] office in Brattle St to see his model of the Foundation Maeght soon to rise among the pines at Juan-les-Pins. This is truly a wonder of the age. A lavish Riviera villa, terraced and planted and dotted with posts to house representative works—presumably for ever—by the living artists who have made Maeght rich: Miró, Léger (now dead), Giacometti, Braque and Chagall. Surely this is the golden age of art dealers. Such is the prosperity, such the snobbism and such the genuine popularity of modern art today

---

18. Josep Lluís Sert (1902–1983) a Catalan architect, was dean of Harvard's Graduate School of Design from 1953 to 1969.

that a dealer can erect this sort of lavish monument to himself. This cannot be called a Museum of Modern Art. It is a museum of success and surely will appear to be an even more peculiar thing as time goes by.

The architecture is ingenious, crisp, modern. But it owes an unexpected debt. The main pavilion resembles nothing so much as a Rajput palace of the eighteenth century as simplified in the miniatures, tile screens, a belvedere with delicate balustrade, decorative panels of colored tiles, the color schemes of red, white, and blue. It also is crowned with an exotic touch. Here they are inverted half cylinders of light concrete poised to catch the rain which in turn spills into a pool. On a lower level are arrayed the humbler buildings—connected pavilions to house the solo displays of each Maeght master, that of Chagall vaguely resembling a chapel to shelter his Biblical series. The ensemble recalls the clustered houses of an Arab village. Romance returns to architecture and a whisper of eclecticism.

1 OCTOBER 1960

Today I delivered the dedicatory address of the new Sawyer Art Center at Colby Junior College, New London, N.H. Across a broad and sunny campus ringed by lofty mountain horizons, we *pro*-cessed and *re*-cessed, the object being the capacious new auditorium. There about five hundred persons gathered to witness the simple dignified ceremony and to listen to me. I am always surprised at my success. My listeners genuinely liked and accepted my thoughts. After I had begun to speak and the audience actually listened, I didn't mind the experience but found the anticipation full of anxiety. I don't often have the opportunity to air my doctor's hoods but today with some pride wore the humane letters from Northeastern.

After retiring at the [Samuel] Bests' comfortable house and rehearsing my speech in bed, found it would not fill the twenty-five minutes allotted me, so, though dead tired I wrote for an hour—enough to occupy eight to ten minutes more, and went to sleep at 1 A.M., wishing I had never got myself into such a pickle. The wonderful [Robert] Baldwins were also houseguests. That fact, my *petit succès*, the exhilarating bright weather and the majesty of the country redeemed the situation and made me happy I had consented to it.

The Ford '36[19] arouses the most extraordinary interest. This time it kept the dinner conversation lively for about twenty minutes. It seems to be the last vestige of motoring as a sport. Without the Ford the drive would have been quite a bore—merely transportation. But the open car, which still looks and behaves like a vehicle instead of a foam rubber armchair encased in metal and mounted on wheels, provides an experience—the means almost justifying the end. I was in the open air for two and a quarter hours, and really felt the contact with nature. And nature today was such as to give you an occasional shudder of delight. Jewel-like patches of color were scattered everywhere and flattered by the bright sun and clear, crystalline air. Occasionally there would be a flash of black water from lake or stream, rippled by the wind and highlighted with sunbeams.

My first visit to the Currier Gallery in Manchester on the return trip. A neat little place with some very good pictures, no

---

19. Rathbone bought his first car in 1936—a battleship-gray convertible 1936 Ford Phaeton that cost $630—when he was assistant curator at the Detroit Institute of Arts. Reluctant to part with this souvenir of his Detroit years, he continued to drive the Ford well into the 1960s, by which time it was an object of curiosity and quite a valuable antique.

sculpture. Especially fine J[acob] Ruysdael, Mabuse portrait, Joos van Cleve, Tiepolo, a not-so-great late Picasso, fine Prendergast watercolor (formally McKean), and excellent Marin watercolor—the kind I would like for MFA.

Dined at the Chilton Club as guest of Mrs. Stanley McCormick[20] and with Bruce Hopper, David McKibbin[21] and Mr. and Mrs. Morton (salt: said he was on a salt free diet!) of Chicago and Santa Barbara. Mrs. McC. alert and eager for every word. Hopper who had a wonderful face and the warmest of smiles was full of original thoughts. Mrs. Morton confessed she was awed at the thought of meeting me! *I* who have been awed at meeting others all my life! But she said she was now completely disarmed and *will* come to see me next time she's in the museum. Mr. M. has no such problem: he *much* prefers talking to listening. Mrs. McC. is the picture perfect of the Boston Dowager who *has* her minks but at eighty-five she is erect and thought nothing of walking back to her house on Commonwealth Avenue with Hopper.

Driving back to Cambridge along the Charles saw the Lowell[22] House Towers lighted for the first time. Hitherto one could forget them by night, now one is reminded late as well as early of the fearful ineptitude of this architectural effort. The riverfront will never again have the harmonious unity it once

---

20. Katharine Dexter McCormick (1875–1967) was among the early female graduates of MIT in 1904 who later helped to fund Margaret Sanger's research and development of the birth control pill.
21. David McKibbin was the author of *Sargent's Boston*, 1956, in conjunction with the exhibition, one of Rathbone's first for the MFA.
22. Rathbone is referring to the Leverett (not Lowell) House Towers, designed by Shepley, Bulfinch, Richardson, and Abbott. Peabody Terrace, designed by Sert, Jackson and Gourley and erected in 1964, would further Sert's vision for Cambridge.

possessed. Behind this monstrous and towering intrusion stands the little, the tiny figure of José Luis Sert and his philosophy that "Cambridge must rise!" The smaller the man the bigger his ambition to impose himself. Cambridge has been marred before but never so irreparably. The miracle is that Cambridge, a city in truth, should have remained in its Harvard precincts anyway a town in outward appearance. This means everything to Americans where too many charming towns have been replaced by cities. But to Sert it means nothing who looks forward to a whole phalanx of towers on the river, who will invest Cambridge with an urban aspect if he can. Sad thing is that he's a fast talker and has [Nathan] Pusey[23] who obviously has no architectural convictions (w. Lowell, for instance), in his pocket. Indirectly Sert is responsible for the intrusion of the Armenian Church: Brattle Street for Harvard supported its effort to change the zoning laws which also permitted the odious towers. Alas for Cambridge.

3 OCTOBER 1960

Last evening we dined with Mrs. Bayard Warren at Pride's Crossing in her big paneled and tapestried house; dark and rich and lofty rooms with immense fireplaces in the high taste of fifty years ago. Mrs. Warren a vivacious and laughing hostess who knows how to move among her guests and make a party "go." Sat at her left and talked much about the museum and her family connections with it. Her grandfather was Francis Bartlett who made the huge "donation" before World War I and

---

23. Nathan Pusey (1907–2001) was president of Harvard from 1953 to 1971.

for whom the "Bartlett Head"[24] is named. Grandpa gave "half his estate" to the museum and made the family furious. Now she's proud of what he did. Cleveland Amory[25] said Bostonians always talked about their grandfathers—from grandpa came all. Her uncle was E[dward] P[erry] Warren[26] by marriage, the one ostracized by all the rest of the tribe because of his "bohemian" life and his absorption with Greek love. Maybe for other reasons too. I don't know. I spoke of the reverence in which he is held by the MFA, and she allowed that she had no quarrel with him. I urged her to come and meet [Cornelius] Vermeule[27] and learn more about E. P. W. Mrs. Warren's pa was Herbert Sears, known for his famous yacht *Constellation*—a ninety-foot boat that carried a crew of thirty-five. Some of his old cronies at dinner told me he usually carried quite a load of whiskey. In any case he looks a rather peevish yachtsman in the Sargent watercolor of him leaning against the main mast of the *Constellation*. His friends claimed that his girlfriend, Mrs. Guy Lowell, appears in the sou'wester in the background.

In the museum at last we are working on the painting galleries, those rooms rendered spiritless and stuffy by W. G. [Constable][28] over twenty years ago. It has taken all the patience I

---

24. *Head of Aphrodite*, also known as "The Bartlett Head," 330–300 BC
25. Cleveland Amory was author of *The Proper Bostonians*, published in 1947.
26. Edward Perry Warren (1860–1928) was a collector of antiquities and outspoken proponent of homoerotic art who gifted much of his important collection to the MFA.
27. Cornelius Clarkson Vermeule III (1925–2008) was appointed by Rathbone as curator of Greek and Roman art at the MFA in 1956 and remained in that position for the next forty years.
28. William George Constable (1877–1976), familiarly known as W. G., was curator of paintings at the Boston Museum from

possess (and have had to cultivate this *active* virtue) to wait five years to do what I most wanted to do. The skylight roof is now re-built at gigantic cost—over $400,000—and the light will be greatly improved. In one gallery we have pulled out dark dado paneling and heavy marble door mountlings. And have had a fabric dyed for the walls. It's just a beginning.

After dinner to the opening of the Robert Light Gallery, Beacon Street alone. Art galleries sprout like mushrooms; this is the latest in Boston. Young Mr. Light, who wears a Lincolnian black beard, has dealt by mail for several years in prints. Now in a deluxe and tasteful atmosphere, his wares from anonymous Italian fifteenth century to Picasso and Braque will be shown to the public, one flight up in a former townhouse. That a fairly expensive address could be maintained on the sale of prints alone would have been in my youth unheard of. Mr. Light has no qualms about the new venture, only great confidence. A small group including Eleanor Sayre,[29] Henry Rossiter,[30] the Dutchman, Begemann[31] were on hand to sip party champagne and look at a really good display.

1938 to 1957. Although he was responsible for important acquisitions such as Renoir's *Danse a Bougival*, he took scant interest in twentieth-century art and, to Rathbone's mind, had an old-fashioned approach to gallery installations.

29. Eleanor Sayre (1916–2001), an authority on Goya's graphic works, was a curator of prints and drawings at the MFA, and was head of the department from 1967 to 1984.

30. Henry Rossiter (1885–1977), was curator of prints and drawings at the MFA from 1923 to 1967.

31. Egbert Haverkamp-Begemann (1923–2017) was at that time curator of prints and drawings at the Yale University Art Gallery.

5 OCTOBER 1960

A usual day with the everlasting and never finished correspondence at the museum. In the evening to Lily Saarinen[32] for
a "cocktail supper" on Brattle Street. She can crowd into her
tiny premises an unbelievable number of people and because
everyone is so closely packed together, it succeeds like a forest
fire. Afterwards to the vernissage of the Egon Schiele exhibition at the Institute of Contemporary Art at the art center on
the Charles. Here was revealed a tense neurotic temperament
of enormous talent—an instinctive expressionist, willing, if not
eager, to reveal the utmost human intimacies using spare bony
models, utterly anti-classical, and for that reason the more red-
olent of nature as she is! One wonders if the Irish Catholic puri-
tans will be outraged by the frankness of these statements—if
they come to look, which is always doubtful, [Thomas] Messer[33]
admitted that the backsides in some of the pictures would really
curl their hair! One wonders whether Schiele would have been
another [Oskar] Kokoschka had he lived. As a draftsman, perhaps. But as a painter he doesn't show that promise. He died at
twenty-eight.

------

32. Lilian "Lily" Swann Saarinen (1912–1995), was a sculptor and
first wife of architect Eero Saarinen. After their divorce in 1954 she
moved to Cambridge.
33. Thomas Messer (1920–2013) was director of the Institute of Contemporary Art from 1956 to 1961. He left Boston to become director
of the Guggenheim Museum in New York, a position he held until
1988.

6 OCTOBER 1960

Spoke before the ladies committee[34] of the museum on modern art in twentieth-century gallery. About fifty bright and eager women seemed to be hungry for all I had to say and took it for about an hour. Confess to be proud of what we have gathered in five years: master works by Picasso, de Staël, Munch, Feininger, Brâncuşi, etc. Spoke about the harbingers of modern outlook: Manet, Whistler, Redon, as well as the more usual Gauguin, Van Gogh, Cézanne. Then lunch in members room surrounded by ladies.

Mlle. Tabarant has accepted our offer on her Manets! Wonderful news. We are blessed to have the patient, intelligent Liliane Jacoel as go between. Our offers: Manet's *Model du bar aux Folies Bergeres* $42,000, *Vase des roses (for Goelet)* $42,000, *Peches (for Mina Curtiss)* $14,000. Tabarant is so pleased she wants Boston to take option on *all* the remaining works which number twelve.

On way home called on old Paul Sachs and gave him an account of my European travels which he listened to with complete absorption. He's a dear old boy who resents being on the shelf. Have not seen him since last Spring and must see him more often.

---

34. The Ladies Committee was a group of volunteers established by Rathbone soon after his arrival at the MFA in 1955, which greatly enhanced outreach, membership, special events, and education. The group has since changed its name to the Associates and is no longer restricted to women.

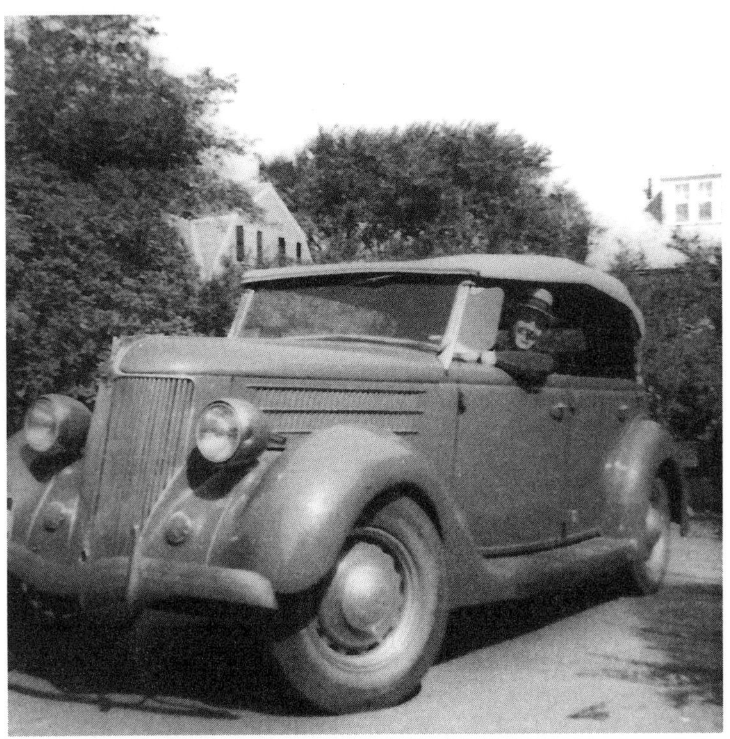

*Rathbone at the wheel of his 1936 Ford Phaeton
in Cambridge, Massachusetts in the 1960s.*

11 OCTOBER 1960

Rather large party for George and Edie Rickey[35] following his lecture at the museum on kinetic sculpture in connection with the current show of modern American sculpture concocted by the Museum of Modern Art. George's presentation left something to be desired: too many "ahems." But his

---

35. George Rickey (1907–2002), then emerging as a leading kinetic sculptor, was a friend of long acquaintance; Edie was his flamboyant wife, secretary, and publicist.

historical justification and rationale for the idea of moving sculpture was convincing, fascinating, especially when illustrated with some of his own works. He refuses to deny nature as a source and inspiration, amen. Audience of one hundred and Bill Dooley[36] the first to congratulate him, thereby gaining full credit for his own presence there! He even brought his wife!

About twenty-five assembled here with emphasis on museum school staff: Coxes (Jan), Coxes (Gardner), Mrs. (Lily) Saarinen, [John] Prip and wife, [Carl] Zahn and wife, Stanley Hausens, Herbert Agooses, Ernest Morenons, Harold Tovishes, Bill Taft (visiting from St. Louis), Larry Longley (from Syracuse), Swarzenskis, and of course Rickeys. Our notable accommodator-butler William Swinnerton[37] and wife made all go smoothly. Long talk with Rickeys afterwards about Curt Valentin of precious memory. Earlier at cocktails and dinner spoke of David Thompson who, to John Coolidge's[38] disingenuous mind is still a hero in spite of having sold his Klee collection—not to an American museum—but to Switzerland and ultimately to Dusseldorf for something like $1,250,000!

13 OCTOBER 1960

Trustees meeting today. A short, not arduous agenda, but a stiff contest to persuade the committee to buy a Whistler! Easier it was to buy a Picasso, a de Staël! "Unfinished" objected Henry Shattuck, an admirable man of the law but possessing

---

36. William Dooley was head of education at the MFA.
37. Swinnerton was a butler for hire trained at Ham House in England who, with his wife, regularly served at the Rathbones' dinner parties.
38. John Coolidge (1913–1995) was director of the Fogg Art Museum at Harvard from 1948 to 1968.

not a fiber of aesthetic sensibility. "Looks as if some boys had scribbled on it!" What does one say and remain polite? This is a red picture. I thought everyone responded to red. All the staff loves this "symphony". The committee showed not the slightest enthusiasm. But by voting myself the picture was bought. Now Whistler as a pioneer colorist is secured for the MFA. This glowing canvas was created ten years before Gauguin started to paint and twenty years before Van Gogh discovered color and its potentialities. But we bought a John Martin[39] *Seventh Plague of Egypt* without much trouble. Only Toledo owns a major work by this artist (Rettles' illustrious great great grandfather) in America.

14 OCTOBER 1960

Today the unexpected pleasure of a visit from Aldous Huxley. He's an immensely tall cadaverous man with a most kind face and gentle manner. His quite unassuming behavior won me at once, never permitting me to feel odd or even self-conscious. We easily fell to talking about pictures in which field he is most knowledgeable and possessed of a keen memory. I showed him the [John] Martin *Plague* in the trustees' room and it fascinated him. When I told him the painter was Ret's great great grandfather he registered surprise at the very thought, saying he never thought of him as being close enough to reality to be the grandfather of anybody! He walks with a curious bending gait, a sort of lope, and he looks at the world through the palest of blue eyes, almost as if veiled with mist. But he wears

---

39. John Martin (1789–1854) was an English romantic painter of spectacular biblical scenes, a contemporary of J. M. W. Turner. He was Rettles Rathbone's great-great-grandfather.

no glasses, only used a loupe from time to time in examining paintings. He was enthralled by the Rembrandts of [Johannes] Elison and wife, and the impressionists, and was impressed by the Ruysdael seascape and the Rubens of Moully [Ahmad] the Arab which he remembered with "total recall" from his previous visit years ago. He was quickly struck by the psychological significance of what he saw: Moully's suspicious eyes, looking away from the spectator as if he expected an assassin, the monstrous idea of a child with his dwarf as in the Velázquez of Don Balthasar, the heinous ceremony of Queen Tomyris bathing Cyrus' head in blood [Rubens]. He was horrified by the colors still left on the walls by W. G. [Constable] and thought he must have been a "sort of negative genius"! Spent an hour and a half with him before I had to leave him a little after mid-day. He is a professor in disguise (his description) at MIT till end of November and delivers a public lecture weekly. So he came with Mrs. John Burchard, wife of Dean of Humanities.

In the evening to the black tie opening of Harvard's new Loeb Theater on Brattle Street. A rather distinguished audience of about five hundred saw *Troilus and Cressida*, a play I will never rush to see again. [Nathan] Pusey, John Mason Brown and Cassie[40], Archibald MacLeish, Don and Zorka Oenslager[41] in attendance. The play has almost no action and many overlong speeches. On the whole well acted by the Harvard dramatic club. But the play was a poor choice for an opener. Pusey made an uninspired and inadequate and offhand speech, never touching on Harvard's great gifts to the American theater, no

---

40. John Mason Brown (1900–1969) was a theater critic, his wife Cassie the former Catherine Meredith.

41. Donald Oenslager (1902–1975), Broadway set designer and founding professor of scenic design at the Yale School of Drama, was Rathbone's first cousin. Ten years his senior, Don was a mentor to Perry, and someone he looked up to in all matters of interior design. Zorka was Donald's ebullient wife.

mention of George Pierce Baker, or any of the vital history that lays behind the new theater. Modest Mr. [John Langeloth] Loeb was commended and received warm applause. Then Pusey sat down and we listened to *T and C* in toto, not a line cut! First act lasted one and a half hours! Theater most attractive and comfortable but too small for Harvard to my mind.

Then Don and Zorka and Cassie Brown here for drinks and merry conversation till 1 A.M. D. and Z. always the most refreshing companions.

24 OCTOBER 1960

Yesterday after church with the girls[42] to the Setons in Concord for luncheon. Sixteen at table including the Bruce Hoppers, Pat Harrisons (Fruitlands Museum, Harvard), Jack Coolidges, Comstocks. Louisa Seton has the gift of making one feel welcome and relaxed in the warm, informal atmosphere of her house typical of so many New England country houses—full of books, much used furniture and slight disorder, a slow fire curling around a log on the hearth, the smell of the roast—back of it all a long tradition of living a civilized life. Then a brief call on the Thompsons nearby to look at an Angelica Kauffmann portrait of East Apthorp's brother and two little children, a covered silver cup and a snuff box belonging to the same.

On the way home we stopped at Orchard house so the girls could soak up the atmosphere of Louisa May Alcott's home life.

---

42. Rathbone's daughters, Eliza, born 1948, and Belinda, born 1950

16 NOVEMBER 1960

Tavern [Club] dinner tonight with Mayor [John F.] Collins as guest of honor and his redevelopment boss, [Edward J.] Logue as principal speaker. Both impressive. Collins spoke from his wheelchair—an articulate, intelligent, and idealistic man who comes as a surprise to Bostonians. He spoke as well, if not even more gracefully and forcefully than he did at the museum luncheon in May. Logue seems to have an "organic" approach to Boston's renewal. Seems genuinely concerned to preserve the best of what Boston possesses. Long talk over beer with Logue and others after dinner until nearly midnight.

Home this morning from trip to Philadelphia, Washington, and New York. Five days away from home. To Philadelphia by night train to appear on two taped programs of *What in the World*[43] with Ted Kidder[44] and Carleton Coon[45] of staff of University Museum on WCAU TV. Guest of Henry McIlhenny[46]

---

43. *What in the World?* was an educational game show hosted by the Penn Museum's director Froelich Rainey that first aired in 1951. Each half-hour weekly program featured objects from the museum's storerooms and challenged a panel of experts to identify them.
44. Alfred Kidder II (1911–1984) was a professor of anthropology at the University of Pennsylvania, a curator of the university museum, and a frequent guest of *What in the World?*
45. Carleton S. Coon (1904–1981), was a professor of anthropology at the University of Pennsylvania and frequent guest of *What in the World?* He was author of many popular books including *The Story of Man* (1954) and the problematic *The Origin of Races* (1962).
46. Henry McIlhenny (1910–1986) was a classmate of Rathbone's as an undergraduate at Harvard as well as in Paul Sachs' museum course. A family fortune derived from his grandfather's invention of the gas meter allowed McIlhenny to begin collecting French paintings and decorative arts at an early age. He was a curator of decorative

in Rittenhouse Square in his luxurious servant filled house. A visit to the closed museum (11 of November legal holiday!) with Henry before lunch. The "improvements" are not to be recorded except as unbelievable. The backgrounds of the [John G.] Johnson collection of paintings remain the same garish pinks, oranges, and greens which quite destroy the paintings that find themselves in so unfriendly a setting.

11 JANUARY 1961

Seems odd not to have Peter[47] home lifting the sports section out of the morning paper as I read it at the breakfast table. I miss his tousled head his rumpled pajamas, his early morning grunts!

Committee meeting today. Not much comment and no spectacular purchases. But yearly records were reviewed: attendance way up: 535,000, highest in years. Membership down a bit, but receipts almost equal to last year. Tom Maytham[48] back from honeymoon in the snowy mountains which he spent flat on his back with the grippe! Instead of skiing with his bride. What a bust!

On way home called on old Paul Sachs at his apartment. Meg and granddaughter there, and Phil Hofer.[49] P[aul Sachs] holds

---

arts at the Philadelphia Museum of Art from the 1930s to the 1960s and later a trustee.

47. Peter is the Rathbones' first-born child and only son, born in 1946. In 1961 he was in his second year of boarding at Brooks School in North Andover, Massachusetts.

48. Thomas Maytham (1931–2019) was assistant curator of paintings under Rathbone. He headed the department after W. G. Constable's retirement in 1957.

49. Philip Hofer (1898–1984) was a collector of rare books and

up very well at eighty-two or eighty-three and is eagerly looking forward to joining committee again in March. He mellows
and is obviously more relaxed now that Meta with her tragic
mental derangement has been carried off. Round about him
having the fruits of years of collecting: his beloved drawings
and objects d'art in a comfortable mélange. Ironic to have sat
next to Phil (Hofer) for his intolerable behavior toward Louis
Stern[50] in the matter of arranging to borrow modern illustrated
books for our show in the spring. But Hofer cannot control
his jealousy and is doing everything to disengage, no alienate,
a true friend of the museum. Departed at 7 and after dinner
packed my bag for two nights in New York.

16 JANUARY 1961

Just home from a gemütlich evening chez [Hanns and Bri-
gitte] Swarzenski:[51] with Eleanor Sayre of our staff and Signora
Todorow [Marquesa Maria Fossi] of the Uffizi here with Italian Drawing Show. Latter is a charming young and intelligent
woman, granddaughter of a Contessa Rucellai, an American

---

founder of the department of printing and graphic arts at the Hough-
ton Library at Harvard in 1938.

50. Louis E. Stern (1886–1962) was an important collector of modern
art and artists' books whose collection, despite Rathbone's efforts,
was mainly given to the Philadelphia Museum of Art and the Museum
of Modern Art in New York.

51. Hanns Swarzenski (1903–1985), a medievalist, was curator of decorative arts and sculpture at the MFA and a close advisor to Rathbone
during his directorship. His wife, Brigitte Horney (1911–1988), was a
German film star, and daughter of Karen Horney, a Neo-Freudian
feminist psychologist. The Swarzenskis were close family friends,
travel companions, and regular guests at feast days.

whose portrait by [Frank] Duveneck I remember seeing in the Palazzo Rucellai a dozen years ago.

The day began with an hour of snow shoveling. A lovely blanket of white has decorated our garden again. But it also fills up our driveway and Ret and I had to clear it before I ventured out. Arranging the Modigliani show most of the time at the museum. One great picture included is the nude from the Joseph von Sternberg Collection. This picture was auctioned in New York about 1948 at which time the St. Louis Museum bid $8,000 which seemed ample to acquire same. But it fell to Museum of Modern Art for record sum of $12,000! Today in our exhibition the painting is insured for $185,000!! But it is a masterwork. This is Modigliani's debut in Boston, forty years after his death and the museum owns no work by the artist. Looking at the exhibition as a whole, he is probably not one of the greatest painters of the twentieth century, but a minor, or secondary master of powerful poetic instinct and a man who knew how to express the pervading sadness of our age.

The great excitement in our domestic and museum circles is the telegraphed invitation to the inauguration of Mr. Kennedy. For the first time cultural leaders are bidden to this event, and should we go? Instinctively I think "yes." Practically the prospect is anything but bright. Who wants to be swallowed up amidst thousands. Who wants to spend time energy and expense with no assurance that anyone would be aware of it? My date in Philadelphia on inauguration conflicts absolutely with the ceremony itself and the parade. I could make the ball only and Rettles is most reluctant hating crowds. But I feel a duty especially as the new president is from Massachusetts. Much, much discussion about problem with Eleanor Sayre, Sgn. T[odorov], and Hanns and Brigitte, all of whom feel strongly we must go: our obligation etc . . . so, we will probably accept with great misgivings. Newspapers are full of forecasts of transportation difficulties in Washington and how does one go to a ball without a hack! But our European friends are shocked that we would hesitate to accept such an invitation because of a parking problem! And they're right!

22 JANUARY 1961

Railroad strikes and a blizzard prevented our going to the inauguration after all. Ret relieved, but I was disappointed having made the resolve. Jane Sabersky[52] stranded here. Snow was still falling thick and fast in A.M. Claude Levy,[53] Ret, and I shoveled driveway and steps, then shoveled again. Museum shut all day. Moved T.V. to drawing room, lit the fire, fetched Jane from the Continental and at noon sipped cocktails as Mr. Kennedy took the oath, Marian Anderson sang the "Star Spangled Banner," Robert Frost read "The Land Was Ours" and all persuasions prayed. Cardinal Cushing gave an embarrassingly long and tedious invocation devoid of all poetry and heavy with cant. Kennedy's speech inspiring, forceful, idealistic, but also realistic. The entire world seems to have responded favorably to his stirring words. His wife looked enchanting throughout.

---

52. Jane Sabersky (1911–1983) met Rathbone while she was an assistant to Curt Valentin in the 1940s. She also worked for the Museum of Modern Art, the Brooklyn Museum of Art, and Vassar College.
53. Claude Levy taught French at the Browne and Nichols School and lived for many years in an apartment above the Rathbones' garage at 151 Coolidge Hill.

28 JANUARY 1961

Just home from a dinner party given by the Stouts at Fenway Court. Cocktails in the gold room where we found the Charles Birds, the Francis Lothrops, Margie [Stout]'s sister Helen and Tom Stout in his uniform of the merchant marine academy at King's Point. President Kennedy's speech continues to reverberate. For it everyone has highest praise. The Lothrops are father-in-law of McGeorge Bundy who goes to Washington from Harvard this week as special assistant to president. Rett looked beautiful in a "new" black dress from Lulu[54] with the "crystal" beads I brought to her from Paris. In fact she was by far the most stylishly dressed lady in the company. Good Liebfraumilch and pleasant conversation.

Tom Messer is leaving us. He phoned to give me the word two days ago. His appointment to the Guggenheim Museum as director will be announced Monday. The honor is richly deserved. He has had to deal with three difficult buildings: Newbury St, quarters in the MFA school, and the new building at the Arts Center.[55] Building problems pursue him for the [Frank Lloyd] Wright museum will hardly be easier premises in which to operate. But he has great pluck, seriousness and high intelligence. I wish him well. And his Philippine wife will be happy. She has never found Boston to her taste.

---

54. As a close friend with a matching dress size, Lulu (Mrs. Joseph) Pulitzer regularly handed down to Rettles her nearly new haute couture.

55. The Institute of Contemporary Art was given its first permanent home on Soldiers Field Road on the banks of the Charles River in Cambridge in 1960 as part of the new Boston Arts Center complex, which included a theater and opera house.

4 FEBRUARY 1961

A sixteen hour blizzard and snow is piled high around us. A drift stands a foot above the windowsill of my study. Ret and I shoveled and shoveled. Three times we cleared the driveway, front and back steps and still there will be more snow to shovel in the morning. But at last the skies have cleared, the moon shines and the stars are out. I have never known such a winter since my childhood—the winter of 1917–18 at Greene[56] when Mother thought we might freeze in our beds and took Weck[57] and me to sleep with her in her bedstead which she had set up in the dining room directly over the furnace! And it has been so cold for days.

Mrs. Kennedy telephoned me this morning from the White House! I couldn't have been more surprised and thought for an instant that someone was pulling my leg. She has artistic ambitions for her new abode and is dismayed at the quality of furniture and pictures she finds there. Ret, busy in the kitchen, dashed upstairs to listen to our conversation. I must say Jackie has a most mellifluous voice and engaging manner. She's utterly relaxed, in no hurry at all and we talked for twenty minutes or so. "Do let me know when you're in Washington again and come to see me." Of course I will. She was enchanted at my offer to lend her from the museum some Sargent watercolors and Dodge McKnights. She wants to give the White House a sort

---

56. Greene, New York, was home to Rathbone's ancestors, both maternal and paternal; the family spent summers and holidays in the house built in 1829 by his great-grandfather Augustus Willard, the village doctor.
57. Westcott "Weck" Rathbone (1909–1987) was Perry's older brother.

of Boston complexion. I was impressed by her ability to convey to a total stranger so much charm and friendliness. Through John Walker of the National Gallery I had made known our willingness to lend to the White House, but I really never expected her to call me. She spoke most enthusiastically about our Prendergast sketchbook and confessed her desire to own a watercolor. I offered to help her. I spoke of our disappointment in not getting to the inaugural ball and couldn't resist telling her how pretty she looked on tv. She replied she didn't see a soul she knew all day long! She asked me to write to her and send photographs of the pictures we might lend.

Dinner last night at the Jim Plauts'[58]. Joe Richardsons, Jack Gardners, Dick Prestons, Charles Francis Adams, Diggory Venns, and Francis Keppels—a lively combination. Long talk with Joe Richardson (grandson of H. H.) about the Leverett House Towers which he has the misfortune to be responsible for. He's a rather erratic, stormy and unbridled sort—stimulating because he is so outspoken, but at the same time boorish. I made no bones about my distaste for his handiwork, but at least could praise him genuinely for insisting his towers be of limestone without brick which would have made them compete even worse with the neighboring house buildings. He's a friend and associate of my long-time friend, Richard Kelly, the lighting expert. A talk with Jack Gardner[59] about new trustees. He's keen to have Hayward Cutting, the Cambridge architect. I would much prefer Jeptha Wade, formally of Cleveland, though I much respect and very much like Cutting with whom

----

58. James Sachs Plaut (1913–1996) was the first director of the Institute of Contemporary Art in Boston, from 1939 to 1958.
59. John Lowell "Jack" Gardner (1923–2021), great-grandnephew of Isabella Stewart Gardner, was a trustee of the MFA during much of Rathbone's directorship.

I have worked on Christ Church architectural problems. Francis Keppel who traveled with Kennedy on campaign told me how much Kennedy disliked Cardinal Cushing, but that for political reasons he simply had to have him officiate at his marriage and at the inauguration. No wonder he looked so pained during that haranguing invocation.

21 MARCH 1961

A long harangue from [Maxim] Karolik.[60] Bob Baldwin and Eleanor Sayre present. Karolik is fearful lest his collection, his "trilogy," should one day not be on exhibition. This is the usual vanity of the collector. But he tries to transpose his vanity to a higher order, to a morality to which we should all subscribe. His view is that he is the savior of these American Arts, once despised, now appreciated, and that our obligation is to provide for their permanent (though rotating) display. The harangue required that we listen to the entire history of the formation of the collection, a story I have heard at least a hundred times in five years.

---

60. Maxim Karolik (1893–1963) was a Russian opera singer who emigrated to America in 1922 and married Boston Brahmin Martha Codman, nearly forty years his senior, in 1928. Karolik's "trilogy" refers to three collections bequeathed to the MFA. To the furniture and decorative arts Codman had already promised, Karolik added American paintings and drawings.

Midnight. Just back from a gathering at Brian O'Doherty's[61] flat in Dartmouth St. in honor of Edward Hopper and his wife who had done a tv program for museum with Brian this evening. Hopper a shy man with a granite-like honesty and few words. He was not at all forthcoming on tv and Brian with all his charm and in-born ability to bring out a personality outdid himself to make a program. Still the integrity, the deep honesty of Hopper was the program. He is not afraid of the homely in his pictures and he is not afraid of the homely in his character. We watched the program here with the Vermeules who were our dinner guests. Hopper on tv reminded Rettles of mother in his shyness, even his balkiness in answering direct questions, in his skepticism and his suspicion of Brian's ingratiating charm. He quoted Goethe who said of true literature that it expressed the outward world in terms of the inward world of the writer. To Hopper the same was true of the true artist. He feels that art is suffering a "depression" today. Spoke warmly of Betty Chace and her genuine love of his pictures. Mrs. H[opper] a volatile and voluble character who added to the tv program.

A letter today from Jacqueline Kennedy inviting me to the White House for sherry on Monday next. Of course I'll go if I can. Her genuine interest in art is a great boon to all of us who are involved with the cultural aspects of American life. Everything this bright and beautiful girl does is of keenest interest to

---

61. Brian O'Doherty (1928–2022), then a youthful Irishman, was host of *Know Your Museum*, one of three MFA programs televised once a week on WGBH at that time. He was also a conceptual artist who went by the alias Patrick Ireland.

the American press. So the MFA loan of eleven pictures to the White House[62] has been reported far and wide.

Yesterday lunched at Mrs. T. Jefferson Coolidge's vast new house at Coolidge Point, Manchester. The house is the quintessence of elegant chi chi, designed by Page Cross, who was a guest—too pink of face and prosperous and spoiled in his expansive plaid suit, too much the darling of his hostess. The typical rich man's architect. Other guests in this extravaganza-by-the-sea (and the view was magnificent) were the Henry Higginsons, Richard Storeys. No works of art of consequence except the historical heirlooms—the five first presidents of Gilbert Stuart and an early watercolor or gouache view of Monticello. Belinda,[63] uninvited, went with us because there was no one to leave her with. And she easily amused herself by exploring the house and gardens and reading her books. A beautiful, sunny, gorgeous day.

12 APRIL 1961

Today I brought home from the museum my great-grandfather's great-grandfather's chair. No one could have been more surprised than I for I didn't even know it was in the museum till the morning. This is the good looking maple Queen Anne style arm chair which belonged to Samuel Willard of Biddeford, Me. Dating from about 1725 in which I sat

---

62. Mrs. Kennedy's "discriminating selection" included a portrait of Daniel Webster by George Healy and watercolors for their private quarters by Winslow Homer, Edward Hopper, John Singer Sargent, and Maurice Prendergast.
63. Belinda is the Rathbones' third child, born 1950.

repeatedly whenever I dutifully called on my spinster distant cousin Theodora Willard in undergraduate days. On each visit to her crowded little apartment in Prescott st. she would tell me that the chair and gate-leg table belonged to Samuel of Biddeford and that she would leave them to Harvard because his son became president of the University. I silently coveted and wondered why she wouldn't consider leaving same to me as she had no heirs. Both pieces were shown in the tercentennial exhibition at Harvard in 1936. In '37 she died. Harvard apparently declined to accept them and they were turned over to the museum. The chair with restored front feet and built-up tack legs was loaned out to the Springfield Museum and only recently recalled. Today at the trustees meeting it was proposed to trade the chair and other articles to the Children's Museum for a screen by Robert Chandler. On Dick Randall's[64] recommendation I noted name of Cousin Theodora and thereby made the identification. The trustees wanted to *give* me the chair, but I prefer to buy it from the museum for its appraised value of $125. Of course I am overjoyed to have this family heirloom from my ancestor who was born in Jamaica and died at an early age. No one can say I am not plain lucky in such matters!

18 APRIL 1961

Yesterday met the President and Mrs. Kennedy. Eliza[65] and I arrived at the White House at 10:30 A.M. At the Southwest

---

64. Richard "Dick" Randall (1926–1997) was assistant curator of decorative arts at the MFA from 1959 to 1964. An authority on medieval ivory carvings, he was director of the Walters Art Gallery in Baltimore from 1965 to 1981.
65. Eliza is the Rathbones' second child, born in 1948.

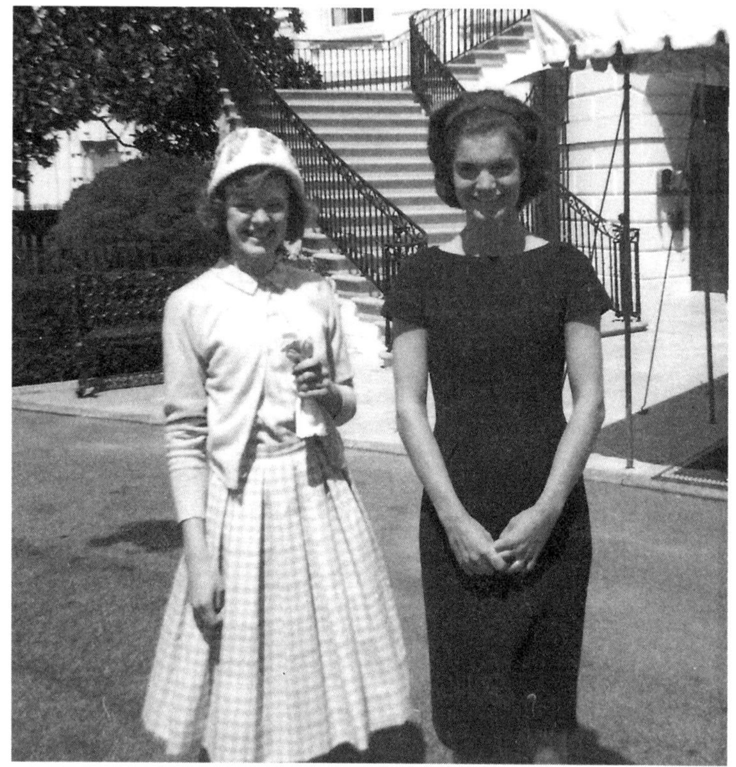

Eliza Rathbone poses with Jacqueline Kennedy
outside the White House in April 1961.

gate our taxi was instructed to drive up to the awning on the South side where we were met by a most congenial colored butler who greeted us by name. An usher soon led us to the elevator and took us to the second floor where we were asked to wait in a passageway room full of [George] Catlin paintings from the Smithsonian collection. The charming Mrs. Kennedy soon appeared. Her ultra simple attire made me feel that I belonged to a different generation. In a way it stated the triumph of the proletariat: a starkly simple dark blue dress, bare arms, no stockings, simple black low heeled shoes, no jewelry. She has hazel eyes, widely spaced under good looking brows. Fascinating rectangular mouth and palest pink lipstick. In all her deportment she was unaffected, graceful, and unselfconscious, but sophisticated. Her voice, low and melodious. A silver head comb drawing her hair back from her forehead held her locks in some control. We sat at west sitting room where she had hung MFA watercolors by Sargent, Homer, Prendergast, and Hopper. They added character and warmth to this lofty, airy chamber where flowered slipcovers and books and overstuffed chairs and sofas gave an air of informality and warmth. Here the Kennedys had recently entertained [Harold] Macmillan.[66] Mrs. Kennedy led us through all the rooms of the private apartment, high ceilinged, light-filled chambers, most of them overlooking the South lawn, the President's bedroom with an enormous four-post bedstead, the "queen's room" which her mother-in-law was soon to occupy, Lincoln's bedroom with its huge dark furniture, an oval drawing room at the center of the house, etc. Then she took us—Eliza speechless with wonder throughout—to the first floor, to the state dining room under preparation for a state luncheon in honor of the prime minister of Greece. Here she had hung the MFA likeness of [Daniel] Webster, the only non-presidential portrait on view in the White House, she pointed out: the red room, green room, and blue room, and finally the East room where we found Mrs. Paul Mellon—a charming person whom "Jackie" greeted with a kiss, calling her an angel for her help. Mrs. Kennedy showed an amazing sense for detail, criticizing the "hotel green" of the dining room which she hoped to have painted white, deploring the recent removal of the Stanford White chimneypiece and

------

66. Harold Macmillan (1894–1986), prime minister of Britain from 1957 to 1963, enjoyed a warm personal friendship with the Kennedys.

its replacement in the Truman administration's renovation by a routine marble fireplace enclosure. The blue room "tragic" to use her favorite adjective, the satin walls with a gold motif are as blue as bluing. The East room has four mantelpieces of liver-colored marble which are about as uninteresting as they could be. Here Mrs. Paul Mellon was busily arranging flowers in honor of the lunch and reception of the Greek Premier. I could only think what a welcome contrast to the florist bouquets which no doubt had satisfied previous first ladies for years untold.

Then to our surprise we were taken in by Mrs. Kennedy to meet the President. He was most genial and quickly observed that I too was wearing a chalk-striped suit. "Same uniform," said he, placing his arm alongside mine. He expressed genuine appreciation for our loans to the White House.

Eliza satisfied her heart's desire by taking Mrs. Kennedy's photograph at the South entrance. She happily posed with me and then I took a snap of Mrs. K and Eliza. Now it was 11:30 and Jackie made her farewells saying she had to have her hair dressed before the Greek luncheon. A White House car was summoned and soon Eliza and I were off to the airport.

Friday the Fuller ball at the Ritz following dinner at the Arthur Brooks in Brattle St. Somehow these debutante parties lack the glamour, the beauty, the "occasion" that they certainly possessed when I was a youth. I suppose the basic reason is that their social meaning is dwindling. I think it is not only because I am older. Certainly I am not cynical or jaded about them. On the contrary I know I could still feel and enjoy the significance of such affairs as a legitimate social event if it were really true.

We left early . . . it was partly because of our depressed spirits. For days we had worried about Peter and the trouble he had got into at Brooks.[67] I had not known such depression for years, and Ret really has suffered. Nothing seems to hit so deep or so hard as matters of honor. It gives untold scope to the imagination . . . and this in spite of similar breeches that I could recall in my own boyhood and that is common enough among all boys.

So to Brooks Saturday morning and a long talk with Mr. Ashburn whose natural sagacity and basic confidence in Peter brought back those cherished feelings about him that we wanted to have. And seeing Peter made all the difference in the world. This, I am sure, has been an important, a maturing episode in his young life. Painful for all but at the same time bringing us all closer together. My heart was lifted and so was Ret's—and I have been a new man ever since.

ATHENS
30 JUNE 1961

Dearest Rett,

I miss you at every turn and can't bear not to have you with me amidst all these first impressions of a new land. And as usual, I seem to have struck it rich. In less than twenty-four hours I have seen the Acropolis by moon light and the King and Queen of the Hellenes. Of course we have seen the [Cornelius and Emily[68]] Vermeules and dined with them the second night at the humble but enchanting garden bistro

---

67. Peter had been caught stealing paperback books from Pop Fryer's village store in nearby West Boxford.
68. Emily Dickinson Townsend Vermeule (1928–2001) was a classics professor and archaeologist who taught at Boston University, Wellesley College, and Harvard.

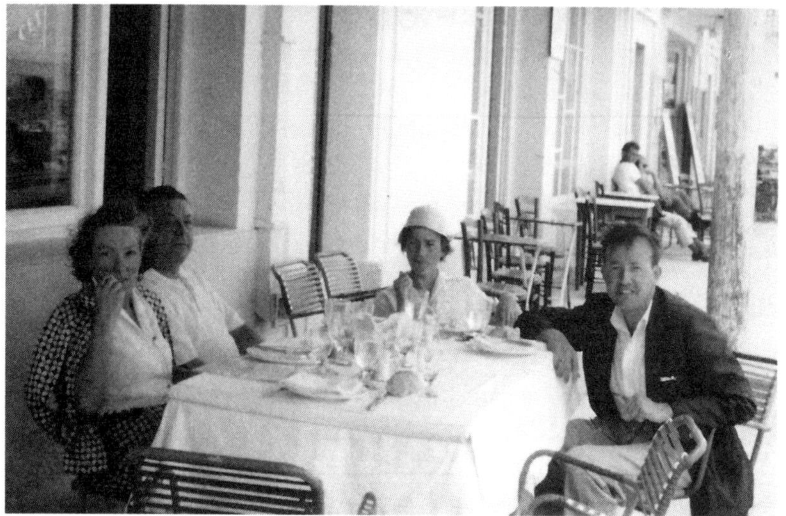

Brigitte and Hanns Swarzenski with Emily and Cornelius
Vermeule pause for lunch in Athens in June 1961.

near the American school where from our table we could look
across the city to the illuminated Acropolis.

But much more important than that was the very first
impression: Hanns [Swarzenski], B[rigitte] and I were alone
our first evening in Athens. The moon was full. After dining
in a viney garden where we drank the delicious wine of
Rhodes, we sought the Acropolis, having been told it was
open. Then, arriving in that precinct, we were told it was
shut. So we consoled ourselves with a bottle of wine at a
humble tavern, resigned to Greek inefficiency in matters
of information. On the point of leaving, Hanns espied two
figures walking within the enclosure, and lo and behold,
there was the gate wide open just beyond where we sat. So we
climbed up through the moonlit groves to that ancient glory
of marble. I could not possibly describe the enchantment
except to say that beyond the expected beauty there was a

nobility, a solemnity and a deeply religious import in that symphony of buildings. The gate through the Propylaeum was locked so H. B. and I hung on the bars in wonder for the best part of an hour, failing in our effort to talk our way in with the guard who, we suddenly realized, had been sitting in the shadow. I believe there is no building in the world to compare with the Parthenon.

Next day we went back and Cornelius gave us a grand tour. He also led us through the Agora and the Agora museum with lovely sculptures and pots, including an ancient Greek toidy! Then a walk through shoe lane crowded with shops like an oriental bazaar and lunch at a workman's bistro where I discovered the most delicious eggplant dish. The Theseion, the Roman forum, Hadrian's Library, the Tower of the Winds, etc., made quite a full day.

Friday we set off on a day motor tour of the Peloponnesus with Corn[elius] and Emily having hired a Peugeot. Can you see us pausing to bathe in the blue waters of the Saronic Bay, lunching on squids at Corinth, exploring the whole romantic ruin of Mycenae with Geo[rge] Mylonas as our guide, poking into the tomb of Clytemnestra and the Treasury of Atreus, then stopping under the vine leaves of an *albergo* for an *orange gazeuse.*

We traipsed over Tiryns with Emily our encyclopedic guide, also full of romantic suggestion. One thinks of the "age of giants" and other such phrases. Of course these ruins are pretty much a matter of one pit after another and I must say that the stones talk in clearer accents to Emily than to the rest of us. She was constantly seeing bronze doors where they did not exist and I teased her a lot about her pits![69]

----

69. Emily Vermeule's *Greece in the Bronze Age* (1964), about Mycenean culture, gave "a sense of the humanity of these people, that these

We came to rest at Nauplia—a most charming fishing village near Argos, dined in the wide open public square under bare electric lights until about midnight. Then slept in our clean, cheap third class hotel. My room was $1.00.

21 SEPTEMBER 1961

Since the last entry here visited eight countries, crossed two continents, swam in three oceans and traveled about ten thousand miles. A bad break for a diary. It exhilarates me to think of standing on the Acropolis of Athens and on the rim of the Grand Canyon in one summer; and to have swum in the Pacific, the Atlantic and the Mediterranean.[70] It is a fair appraisal to say that the Parthenon is the greatest wonder by the hand and mind of man, the canyon the greatest wonder of nature.

1 OCTOBER 1961

Today, Sunday, we folded up at the Cape,[71] packed up bedding and provisions and motored home in both cars in bright dry weather. Belinda and Susan Forbes in my car, Eliza and Barbara Peabody in Ret's. Hanns and Brigitte Swarzenski fol-

---

were not just pieces of pottery on the ground." Cynthia Shelmerdine, *Harvard Gazette*, 2001.

70. Rathbone met his family in California during their transcontinental tour in the summer of 1961.

71. Beginning in the mid-1950s the Rathbones rented a simple beach cottage from Perry's cousin Beatrice "Betty" Oenslager (Mrs. Malcolm) Chace (1905–1992) at Great Island, the Chace family's private enclave in West Yarmouth, Massachusetts.

lowed in their Volkswagen. A weekend of perfect weather and the Swarzenskis perfect guests. The swimming was for the gods: cold, clear, bracing water and lively surf giving us magnificent appetites for buckets of freshly gathered mussels. Ret, Brigitte and I swam this morning before breakfast; then the Swarzenskis and I had a last lovely swim before leaving this P.M.

Our cottage "no. 6" still surrounded by vast drifts of sand swept up from the beach by Hurricane Esther. Learned from Jay Stratton[72] of MIT that Esther had been "seeded" by high-flying planes thus dissipating its destructive force just off Cape Cod. Otherwise our cottage would surely have been blown to pieces. But this is confidential information not released by government. Dined Saturday night with Malcolm and Betty Chace at the big house, the six of us having a gourmet repast prepared by Malcolm.

13 OCTOBER 1961

Budget meeting today with B[ob] Baldwin and Ned Humphrey and I recommended raising our senior curators to $12,000—a new maximum and still not high enough in my opinion. But it begins to be respectable. I recommended raises all along the line, but I fear it is always the lower echelons—who get first consideration. We are blessedly free of unions and want to stay that way. We have an exceedingly "happy ship" and I have no complaints. The only unsatisfactory performance is that of [William] Dooley who is beyond habituating himself to effective functioning. Rum and laziness.

---

72. Julius Adams "Jay" Stratton (1901–1994) was president of MIT from 1959 to 1966.

Nine Fuller[73] paintings, gifts at long last of the Foundation are now on splendid view enhanced temporarily with red drapery backgrounds in the stately gallery around the stairs. This the triumphant close of a long, anxious and often painful campaign commencing six years ago with W. G. Constable's low grade effort to discourage me from obtaining anything from the Fullers. This may have reflected his own lack of success with the governor. But the exhibition nearly three years ago set us on the right road. The strange and unaccountable suspicions of the fatherless family were gradually allayed and we ingratiated ourselves by providing storage rooms for entire collection when the Beacon st. house was emptied, by offering advice for dispersal, cleaning etc. Three paintings were originally offered: Van Dyck, Romney *Lady de la Pole*, and Renoir *Canotiers*! Thus I made a plan for four more: Romney, *Thornhill*, Reynolds *Fitzpatrick* Monet *Water Garden* and Boucher *Shepherd Boy*. At a meeting of the family foundation at the Algonquin Club the day before I flew to Europe I was unexpectedly summoned and was most kindly interrogated by Alvan Jr on my request. This was then agreed upon and to my amazement I was asked to select two more pictures for the museum. I named the Boccaccio Boccaccino and the Renoir *Dominos*. Half an hour after I returned from the meeting Alvan rang up to say that all six pictures would be added to the original three! The one great regret is the Rembrandt about which I had written the most persuasive letter I could compose. But Peter Fuller, it turned out, stubbornly insisted upon buying it from the Foundation

---

73. Alvan Fuller (1878–1958) made a fortune as an automobile dealer and once served as governor of Massachusetts. With his fortune he amassed a sizeable collection of European paintings. After Fuller's death Rathbone courted his descendants for further important gifts to the museum.

for himself and against all the arguments of the family. We can only hope that he may one day give it.

My fourth gallery talk today on the first eight galleries of paintings to be renovated. My audiences have loved the subject as they genuinely love the changes that have been made. Many believe all the paintings have been cleaned. Some have; but it is primarily the light, the backgrounds, the harmonious arrangements that have made the difference. We have rehung two hundred pictures in the year. It begins to look like a new museum!

Peruvian show is a great beauty and all thanks to Dus Cavallo[74] and Hanns—paragons of taste and hard work and selfless devotion. We had eighteen guests for dinner prior to the opening: [Dudley T.] Easbys from the Metropolitan and [Frederick] Dockstaders from the Heye Foundation in New York. Robert Moores, Swarzenskis, Bob Gardners, Samuel Lothrops, Dave Littles, José Luis Serts, and Dr. [Jorge C.] Muelle, Director of the National Museum in Lima, Peru. A rather odd mixture which, I think, finally jelled. Swinnertons as usual managed all and Eliza opened the door.

19 OCTOBER 1961

Ret and I home from our travels this P.M. by New Haven train. I left last Sunday morning by train to Philadelphia to do two TV programs on tape for University Museum at WCAU. Paused for half hour at Philadelphia Museum to observe "improvements" to the painting galleries. They seem to have succeeded in making them look permanently temporary. Not one revamped room has become an architectural entity: the

---

74. Adolph "Dus" Cavallo (1926–2022) was curator of textiles at the MFA.

floors remain concrete, there is no finishing moulding at baseboard or ceiling and while wall colors are less screamingly garish, they have no pleasing texture. None of the pictures are arranged with even a semblance of grace and harmony while the great Brâncuşi collection of [Louise and Walter] Arensberg is dissipated throughout a number of galleries.

Tough but amusing program of *What in the World* television with Ted Kidder and Carl Coon and Fro Rainey[75] as "interlocutor." All of us stumbled on the Venetian gondola oarlock—a new one in raw walnut—and declared same to be a modern abstract sculpture!

To Washington Monday morning to lunch with Mimi[76] in the dining room. But sadly Mimi has failed considerably and in spite of her valiant effort to keep up her condition is quite pitiful. Dressed and to Baltimore by train for opening of Van Gogh show. Mr. and Mrs. Van Gogh very smilingly on hand. At head table Ret sat next to Dean Acheson and I next to Mrs. A who turns out to be granddaughter of John Mix Stanley, the Indian painter. Ret reported Acheson to be very negative about present administration and pessimistic about any lasting world organization that would outlaw war. Thought Kennedy talked too much and that his Harvard "Brain Trust" would do much better at the University!

Wednesday A.M. met Hanns [Swarzenski] at Downtown Gallery and selected an Arthur Dove watercolor and a fine collage,

75. Froelich Rainey (1907–1992) was host of the television program *What in the World?* and director of the Penn Museum.
76. Mary Amelia "Mimi" Kirkbride Peckitt (1879–1968) was Rettles' aunt whose ample townhouse in Washington, DC, provided a family base in that city.

Long Island and two [John] Marin watercolors. But also had to listen to boastful monologue of Edith Halpert for two hours.

24 OCTOBER 1961

Cleaning of Degas' *Carriage at the Races* is completed. This small masterwork is now a pearl. From under an old veil of discolored varnish and dirt emerges a landscape with figures bathed in clean air, a sky dotted with tiny puffs of vapor, a vast sweep of field of a tender indescribable green. The sunshine described is soft, luminescent. This is surely one of the triumphs of "plein airisme" without reliance on the impressionist technique of broken color. Bought for $30,000 in 1926 by the museum, it is surely worth $230,000 today. Work has begun on cleaning the "jockeys",[77] another tiny jewel of the collection, acquired in 1903 for $9,000. The rather seriously crackled sky has been over-painted with a deep creamy color which John Finlayson is now removing to reveal a sky of pinkish purplish tint which has form and air.

25 OCTOBER 1961

John Pope[78] and I spent an hour and a half in the bowels of the Asiatic department examining the celebrated Japanese erotica collected by Dr. [William Sturgis] Bigelow.[79] I was amazed

---

77. *Racehorses at Longchamp*, Edgar Degas (1871)
78. John Pope (1906–1982) was an authority on Asian art and was soon to become director of the Freer Gallery in Washington, DC.
79. William Sturgis Bigelow (1850–1926) was one of the three Boston collectors of Japanese art that made the MFA's collection the

not only by the often violent content of the material but by the quantity. Several hundred books (from the humblest "paperbacks" to the most elegant) and scrolls from the sixteenth to the nineteenth century. Much of the erotica is delightfully humorous and much of it is extravagant beyond imagining. We could only examine a fraction of it all in one and a half hours. Tomorrow a photographer from the Kinsey laboratory of sex studies in Bloomington, Indiana (U of Ind.) commences months of work in photographing the entire collection. The university has asked to take it all on permanent loan but to this I objected and proposed the photographs which should serve their purpose—whatever it is.

Then John and Hanns [Swarzenski] and I attended a Bordeaux wine tasting party at the Ritz and had a lovely time sampling nine chateau wines. Most surprising, delightful and different was a Vieux Chateau Certan 1955 Pomerol. Could one call it many faceted?

26 OCTOBER 1961

Woke up in the night, a frequent occurrence of late and found it hard to sleep, my mind revolving around the little cleaned Degas paintings, the appearance of the galleries when installed, and other aspects of the grand renovations now underway. Unfortunately, I can see these galleries as if I were in them, every detail. It is inimical to sleep.

---

most important outside of Japan. Bigelow's taste for the vernacular traditions (including erotica) stood him apart from his fellow collectors, Edward Sylvester Morse and Ernest Fenollosa, both of whose research he helped to fund.

The Vincent W. Van Goghs[80] for dinner with the Swarzenskis. Most gemütlich evening. Ret roasted a leg of lamb and to it I added the white Chianti which was a mistake. Nevertheless a good dinner and most convivial. Mrs VG a fun-loving soul and both most at home in America. They are following Baltimore opening and on route to New Hampshire to visit friends. While Van Gogh is elderly with a lined face and white hair, his resemblance to his uncle is very marked. Both he and his wife wear the mantle of their distinction lightly. Both were very appreciative of the "collection" *chez nous.*

28 OCTOBER 1961

Yesterday morning hurried to the museum to meet Mr. and Mrs. David Bakalar[81] at 9:30 to show them a fine Kokoschka and recommend the purchase of same; but principally to ask him to buy the Erickson Rembrandt of Aristotle[82] at the forthcoming sale for my estimate at $1,500,000. In the spring he told me he *could* do it but upon pressing the matter simply by saying it wasn't a Rembrandt that appealed to him personally subjectively! I tried to persuade him on grounds that it would be a disgrace should the painting leave the US, that it would be great for Boston, and that it was a miracle that such a painting should even be offered for sale in this age. But to no avail. At least I

---

80. Vincent Willem Van Gogh (1890–1978) was the artist's nephew and the founder of the Van Gogh Museum in Amsterdam, which opened in 1973.
81. David Bakalar (born 1924) founder of the Transitron Electronic Corporation, became an avid art collector and took up sculpture at the age of sixty-two.
82. Rembrandt's *Aristotle with a Bust of Homer* was soon to be auctioned off at Parke-Bernet in New York.

had the satisfaction of seriously asking him to spend 1.5 million for a painting. Mr. B declared his interest in a self-portrait, so have written to [Edward] Speelman to inquire about the beautiful rediscovered work he showed Hanns and me in London last summer. Of course David B[akalar]'s millions (reputed 50 to 100) are very new: too new to spend on Rembrandt of great price, perhaps. The other Boston millions are too old. What a predicament.

29 OCTOBER 1961

End of daylight savings and all of us up an hour early having forgotten to turn back the clock last night. To church with the girls and in plenty of time for once! After dinner with B[elinda] to Waltham to see Gore Place, an unusual and graceful Federal mansion which I had seen only once before at a large reception. Oddly, an anonymous work but thought to be designed by an Englishman. B. most observant and delighted with the house and everything in it. She is by far the most visual of the children and easily expresses her opinions and her many enthusiasms. Eliza at thirteen is just moving into the self-conscious age. She's very pretty and popular but inimical to boys and rather dreads her first mixed dinner party next week. Afterwards paid our first visit to Brandeis and specifically to the Rose Art Center—a big cube of dressed stone and glass on two levels containing the initial stage of the permanent collection—a rather sad array of undistinguished paintings and a collection of English pottery. Lower floor surrounding a pool contained loan show of modern European abstract paintings. Then home for tea and a little family celebration of B's eleventh birthday. A stamp album and a recorder made her very happy and she lost no time in playing on the one and pasting in the other.

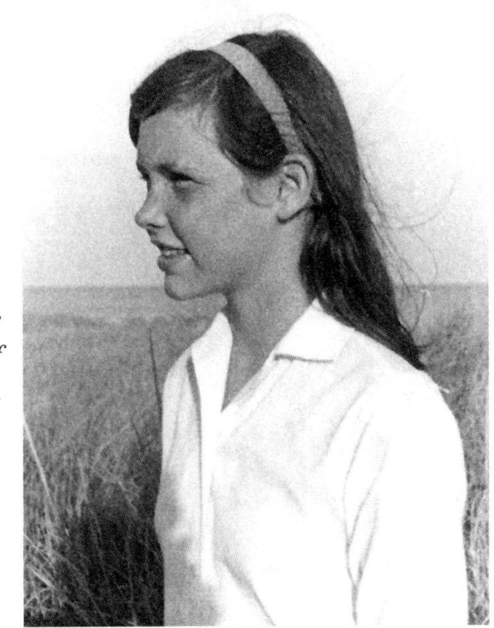

Belinda Rathbone enjoys the last of summer on Cape Cod, c. 1961.

17 NOVEMBER 1961

Endless interruptions today. So many in fact that I got only two letters written and came home with a briefcase full to work on over the weekend. Trustees full board meeting yesterday and afterwards a tea for new members at which I conducted a large party through the newly renovated painting galleries. Many favorable comments about the work to date.

But the week began with unforgettable events: dinner at the White House Monday night and the record breaking auction in New York Wednesday night.

Ret and I took the night train to Washington Sunday, had a visit with Mimi in the morning, then to the Corcoran to see the Civil War Show with H[ermann] W. Williams. Lunch with

Kate Davis Quesada in her new house in Kalorama Circle. Still complaining about not having enough pictures having missed countless opportunities since she first recognized her need. But she was in fine form, her usual entertaining and charming self. Very amusing about brother, Joe Pulitzer, who was so enthralled by the entertainment at the White House last month.

In the afternoon we simply rested at Mimi's preparing ourselves for the big event of the evening. In my new London tails for the first time (what lucky timing to have ordered them) and Rettles in her ravishing ashes of roses ball dress of last Christmas and a few—not too many—family diamonds and the amethyst and diamond pin from Venice, and Mother's long white gloves years and years old, we set out for the White House having passed careful inspection by Mimi and her nurse. Among the first to arrive, we were escorted to the East room, Ret on the arm of a Marine usher and our names were sounded on the loud speaker as we entered. By 8 o'clock the stately room was comfortably filled with the President's 150 guests in grand terrace drinking cocktails. Then a flourish of trumpets and other instruments and down the hall advanced a marine color guard at a solemn pace. At the doorway they stood aside and as an usher's voice was heard to say, "the Governor of Puerto Rico and Madame Marín, the President of the U.S. and Mrs. Kennedy," they appeared and smiled at their guests. We had meantime formed a circular double line to be received, the gent preceding the lady. The President greeted me warmly and said "I'm glad to see you <u>again</u>" by which I was consciously flattered. Mrs. Kennedy looked entrancing in a green chartreuse column of silk with leaf-shaped diamond pins encircling her top-of-the-head chignon. Her slender figure was in contrast to the dumpy form of Madame Marín; but the latter was geniality itself. All this went off with admirable smoothness, and while necessarily formal and even pompous at moments, one felt a friendly informality gradually taking over the entire function. My eye was attracted by an enormous and gorgeous bouquet of chrysanthemums in an urn opposite the entrance to the East room and didn't fail to notice that the four liverish mantels of the Truman reconstruction had been camouflaged to look like grey veined white marble. Ret's table with ten others was in the State dining room where the President sat while I was in the Blue room with five tables next to Mrs. Kennedy's table. Light blue tablecloths, candlelight and charming bouquets, a blazing fire on the hearth, President Monroe's gold table service—all this gave the room a festive, warm, and inviting atmosphere, which was brought to the highest pitch with dessert when the Air Corps "singing strings" (eight or ten good fiddlers) surrounded the room and played away in a grand serenade of the guests. At my right Mrs. Friendly, with a managing editor of the *Washington Post*, then Mayor [Robert] Wagner of New York. On my left Robert Dowling, big wheel financier of New York, real estate operator and head of the proposed cultural center for Washington. Across from me sat Mrs. David Dubinsky, wife of the garment workers labor organization looking, poor thing, quite bewildered and ignored by her table companions. One was Edwin Pauley, powerful Democrat from Los Angeles. He overheard me say to Mrs. Friendly that I thought the Erickson Rembrandt would fetch two million and afterwards buttonholed me to say he wanted to do all he could for Ric Brown, director of L.A. Museum. But he added he could do a million, but he didn't see how he could go to two! Dinner was excellent, especially a mousse of fish to begin with and a pheasant pâté with the salad. Three wines—two California, of fine vintage, and Champagne. Ret fared better with table companions than I did. With T[homas] J. Watson of IBM on one side, Mr. Friendly on the other, and next but one to Mrs. Auchincloss who proved to be most charming. After dinner we filed back into East room for the [Pablo] Casals concert, which was glorious. He seemed especially fine in the Couperin, the breadth of his tone and virile strength of his bowing brought forth sounds that could only be compared with the whole string section of a superlative orchestra. Sitting in the grand room with pretty Ret on my right and Gian Carlo Menotti and Leonard Bernstein on my left, William Paley and Mrs. Auchincloss just beyond, [Leopold] Stokowski standing against the wall, and a glittering company all around absorbing great sonorous music from a great artist, I was conscious of my privilege every moment. The President spoke with simplicity and sincerity about the artist in a free society before the concert. We talked with Menotti about Spoleto, with the Henry Fords about the Rembrandt, which Mrs. F said she was going to buy—and with real determination; with the Roger Sessions, Elliott Carters, and Walter Lippmanns. Rather expected some other museum directors, but there were none. After the concert, about 11:30, we took our departure and having failed to order a car, Ret and I simply sauntered off in our evening attire into the balmy clear night leaving the White House grounds by the Southwest gate until we hailed a cab in Farragut Square and rode home.

An early plane to New York to lunch with Quappi Beckmann[83] at the St. Regis, where Joe Pulitzer was to have enter-

---

83. Mathilde "Quappi" Beckmann (1904–1986) was the widow of Max Beckmann, who died in 1950. Rathbone helped the Beckmanns emigrate to the United States from Amsterdam in 1947 by securing Max a teaching position at Washington University in St. Louis, when Rathbone was director of the City Art Museum. The two couples became close friends, and after Max's death Perry was a constant consultant to Quappi in matters of her estate.

tained us but then disinvited us. Q. wanted to discuss her will and the Beckmann paintings and sculpture—of the first importance—she intends to leave to the MFA. She was well and looking very pretty. Drink with the Queen[84] at Carlton house and then to a party at the Hanns Schaeffers before going to the Rudolf Heinemanns for dinner. An excited company of about twenty in honor of Baron and Baroness Thyssen including the Jack Heinzes from Pittsburgh, the [James] Rorimers,[85] and Severance Millikins, and others from Cleveland seeming very confident about the sale on the morrow. Mrs. M's diamonds seeming to announce the financial power of the Cleveland faction! As it turned out the three chief contenders for *Aristotle* were there: Thyssen, Cleveland, and the Met. Heinemann was in a high state of excitement. After many drinks we transferred to the Cote Basque Restaurant in 55th street and had a gala dinner. I sat next to Baroness Thyssen, across from Mrs. M and her diamonds, and having Mrs. [Eugene] Thaw on my right. New Yorkers are so often ignorant of Boston that I am compelled to suppress modesty and extol the wonders of the MFA.

Spent the night in Carlton House suite thanks to hospitality of M. Knoedler. Breakfast at Schrafft's and then met Sally Kerr settling into quarters I was prepared to quit in the evening.

Saw Hirschl and Adler in the A.M. who agreed upon a thousand dollars for *News Boy* by Fred[erick] Spencer. Meantime I have also decided to buy from [Giovanni] Castano Childe Hassam watercolor of rocks and sea (1912) for $1,800, a painting formerly in Governor Ely's collection. Extravagant, yes; but I would only reproach myself in future if I failed to buy it.

---

84. "The Queen" was Rathbone's nickname for Jane Sabersky.
85. James Rorimer (1905–1966) was director of the Metropolitan Museum of Art from 1955 to 1966.

Lunched with Tom Howe[86] and Otto Wittmann[87] as executive committee of AAMD (American Association of Museum Directors) at Plaza in the Oak room. Restored by the Bloody Mary cocktails but depressed by poorly cooked bluefish. Settled on Sarasota for meetings next year, discussed tax problems and drive for museum thirty percent income deduction. Also discussed Barbizon exhibition which will be shared by Toledo, San Francisco, and Boston. To Wildenstein in P.M. Saw beautiful Bonnard (1907) of Natanson girls for $150,000. Drinks with the Weils and Gordon Washburn and joined by John Wilson of Brookline before the latter as my guest and I took off at 7:00 for the great sale. At Parke-Bernet we stood amongst a mass of people holding preferential tickets at 77th street entrance for a half hour before being admitted to a sales room nearly filled. Got last group of seats in a room replete with all the greats of the country's art world. Atmosphere electric, of course. By time of the sale, everyone in New York was sure it would be two million for the Rembrandt. John Wilson on my left absorbed the atmosphere with great gusto. David Pleydell-Bouverie[88] and Tom Howe on my right, Harry Francis of Cleveland immediately in front of me. In a short time the R. was before us on the stage and after a harangue by auctioneer [Louis] Marion the bidding began at one million. In four minutes it was over with the Met as winner of this world contest. With Rosenberg and Stiebel as agent, Cleveland was underbidder. And this is as it should

---

86. Thomas Howe (1904–1994) was director of the California Palace of the Legion of Honor in San Francisco from 1939 to 1968.
87. Otto Wittmann (1911–2001), director of the Toledo Museum of Art from 1959 to 1976, was Rathbone's Harvard classmate and co-director of the Harvard Society of Contemporary Art.
88. David Pleydell-Bouverie (1911–1994), an English architect deeply interested in nature conservation, bought more than five hundred acres in Sonoma Valley as a nature preserve.

have been—the two richest museums of the US vying with one another, the richer the winner. I observed [Charles] Wrightsman in the second or third row, flanked by Ted Rousseau and [James] Rorimer, so the determination of the Met was fairly obvious at a glance. But I believe Los Angeles was also in the contest, what with [Edwin] Pauley's million and Ric Brown[89] looking confident in the front row. A burst of applause greeted the conclusion of the Rembrandt sale—the highest price ever paid for a painting.[90] Actually, considering inflation the interest on Erickson's investment, this was only a small advance over the price of $750,000 which he paid [Joseph] Duveen in 1924.

26 NOVEMBER 1961

Returned last night from Thanksgiving weekend in Greene with Weck and his family.[91] Leaving Cambridge Wednesday P.M. drove as far as Springfield on the turnpike and then rendezvoused with Ellie and Tam transferring to Weck's big Mercury station wagon. This gave Peter an opportunity to keep the girls in an uproar for the six remaining hours of the journey. But a few quiet moments while he gave each of them a logic-perception and info test he had brought from school. Weck had all the preparations under his command including a marvelous great kettle of vegetable soup; the table was set and the

89. Richard "Ric" Brown (1916–1979) was director of the Los Angeles County Museum of Art from 1962 to 1966, and became the first director of the Kimbell Art Museum in Fort Worth in 1966.
90. $2,300,000
91. Perry's brother Westcott took over the ancestral house in Greene, New York, after their mother died in 1960. Eulalie was his second wife and Tamasin was his daughter by a previous marriage.

twenty-two-pound turkey ready for the all-night oven. Thanksgiving day we had a great feast. The great bird was a notable success and the Vouvray and champagne much appreciated. There were mountains of fruit on the table and afterward port and nuts in like abundance. Long private conversation with Weck about dividing the choicest of the family heirlooms, I taking the position that I wanted to enjoy our family things at home throughout the year, Weck reluctant to deprive the old house of anything it contained. We discussed a list I had prepared of the silver, porcelain, the tea sets, girandoles, candlesticks, bronze lamp, samplers, family prints, and pictures etc. but little progress by the time we retired about 2 A.M. Rain on Friday so a good day to clear out safe deposit box at the bank instead of shooting at the Marcy farm. Spent the morning in the front room (what Belinda calls the "evening room" as opposed to the morning room) dividing the family jewelry, watches, lorgnettes, keepsakes etc and all the silver which mother had not designated for each of us. Found that several pieces of silver had disappeared, including the Dederer Sheffield cake basket and wine coaster and coffee pot. As a boy of six I had observed in the same house a similar scene in 1917 after my grandmother's death when her jewelry, diamonds, china and other valuables were divided between Aunt Jane and Mother and Uncle Jim flipping the coins for first choice. It took place in the upstairs hall and the event is as vivid as if it had happened yesterday. I found my own experience somewhat of a strain and certainly the division was fraught with deliberation, especially on Weck's part.

28 NOVEMBER 1961

Sandy [Alexander] Calder at museum today and Louisa, but alas, too busy to see him. Cocktails at the J. L. Serts in honor of Calders. Long talk with Lee Gardner[92] about Bob G[ardner][93] who flew to New Guinea at request of Nelson Rockefeller to help search for Michael R[ockefeller] lost on treacherous North coast of island.[94] Met an attractive Pole, Mr. Soltan, an architect at school of design with Serts. Reluctantly sped away from this large and merry group to dine with Alden McIntyre at 100 Memorial Drive. Met the attractive young Spaldings and had long talk with Mrs. S about Jackie Kennedy whom she knew well at school. She reported Jackie was always two jumps ahead of everybody—artistically, intellectually, and that all her friends were frankly jealous of her for her beauty, precocity, and genuine artistic tastes and insight.

---

92. Ainslie "Lee" Anderson Gardner was Bob Gardner's wife; they were later divorced.

93. Robert Gardner (1925–2014), a collateral descendent of Isabella Stewart Gardner, was a documentary filmmaker and anthropologist who was founder and director of the film study center at Harvard from 1956 to 1997. In 1961 he traveled to New Guinea to make his film *Dead Birds* about the Stone Age Dani tribe, with twenty-three-year-old Michael Rockefeller as his sound editor.

94. Michael Rockefeller (1938–1961), son of Nelson Rockefeller, was lost on Papua, New Guinea, having traveled there in October 1961 to study and collect artifacts of the Asmat tribe. The Asmat were known to still practice cannibalism, and it was conjectured that Michael had been their victim. His body was never found.

29 NOVEMBER 1961

Visit from Sandy and Louisa Calder. Sandy is as big and burly as ever, but now white of hair. Red shirt, orange tie. His blue eyes are alternately innocent, ingenuous, almost child-like, and keenly intelligent and shrewd. Led him to his own works in museum of which there are four plus my own loan of a mobile. He quickly fixed the wire cow[95] and with a bit of copper wire provided it with a dropping which he said was missing from his original design!

Charlie Peterson of Philadelphia for lunch and a meeting of a citizens committee for preservation of Old Boston at Athenæum. About forty in attendance presided over by Walter Whitehill.[96] This is really the outgrowth of luncheon meeting at MFA a year ago last May when we gathered at one table, politicians and preservationists. Then tea at Mrs. Evelyn Sears, 85 Mount Vernon Street to see the objects she wishes to leave to MFA. A fine Bulfinch house overlaid heavily with Victorian taste. Miss Sears a spry eighty-four years. Then press party at museum for Chinese show long enough to drink a couple of martinis and talk with newspaper, tv, and radio people. House and change for dinner with John Bullards at Chilton Club to see movie of panorama of New Bedford and whaling round the world. Sat next Mary Hyde, guest of honor, and Mrs. William Aldridge. Large party of eighty and much fun.

---

95. Calder's *Vache (Cow)* (, c. 1929) was acquired by the MFA in 1960, with the "dropping" added in 1961.
96. Walter Muir Whitehill (1905–1978) was director of the Boston Athenæum, a trustee of the MFA, and author of the centennial history in 1970. A staunch advocate for preservation, he declared the construction of the twelve-story Ritz Carlton Hotel in the Back Bay in 1927 "the point of no return."

2 DECEMBER 1961

Opened Chinese show[97] on 30th with some fanfare. Dinner for ninety-three in big impressionist gallery with Minister Chiang[98] [representative ambassador Yeh] and Madame Chiang as guests of honor. Sat next to Madame Chiang and Mrs. [Sidney] Rabb[99] and Ret sat next to [Aschwin] Lippe of Met and had a good time. Ralph Lowell[100] made brief speech of appreciation, but referred three times to Chinese exhibition of "portraits." Subconsciously, I suppose the proper Bostonian equates portraits with paintings. Chiang also spoke and for once I was able to keep still—at my own insistence. Following excellent dinner, we filed into tapestry hall at 9:30 and found it overflowing with eager crowd which before evening was over swelled to highest opening reception crowd on record—over 3,300. After exhausting forty-five minutes in receiving line brought home for nightcaps Schwin Lippe and Hanns, the Maythams and Bart Hayes[101] and wife and eldest daughter. After others had retired had long political discussion with Schwin about

---

97. *Chinese Art Treasures* presented 253 works of calligraphic and decorative arts loaned from the Chinese government in Taiwan.

98. Chiang Ching-kuo (1910-1988) was the son of Chiang Kai-shek and his successor as the leader of the Republic of China in Taiwan. At the time of this writing he was Minister without Portfolio.

99. Sidney Rabb (1900–1985) owner of Stop & Shop and other chain stores, was a patron of the MFA.

100. Ralph Lowell (1890–1978), a banker and prominent Boston philanthropist, was president of the MFA's board of trustees at the time of Rathbone's appointment in 1955 and served until 1968.

101. Bartlett Hayes (1904–1988) was director of the Addison Gallery of American Art at Phillips Academy, Andover, and a champion of modern art.

American democracy and freedom and American determination to preserve same.

6 DECEMBER 1961

Things have quieted down a bit since the Fogg visiting committee weekend. That is, we are not busy every minute. But this P.M. late Hanns [Swarzenski] and I went to reception for new director Institute of Contemporary Art, Mrs. Sue Thurman at the Institute. Mrs. Thurman with orchid and warm smile seemed to me to be the very soul of self-assurance. Well she might be as there seems to be plenty to relieve her attractive face quickly of its smile: the clouded future of the arts center of which Institute is integral part and very serious deficit. The two former directors present, Tom Messer and Jim Plaut and the usual attractive Institute group amidst a rather bewildering array of contemporary Italian sculpture. W. G. Constable on hand. What does he do? Although retired and living on an MFA pension he has not been seen in the museum for any purpose since he left four years ago. But affairs concerning contemporary art, in which he hasn't the slightest interest or understanding, he busily attends. He stated that a purchase at Sotheby's today of a "potato eater" Van Gogh portrait of a woman for 8,000 pounds was a poor purchase!

Great dissatisfaction revealed at Fogg meetings with Harvard's lackadaisical campaign to raise funds for I Tatti.[102] Henry McIl-

---

102. Villa I Tatti is Harvard's Center for Italian Renaissance Studies in Florence, Italy, formerly the home of Bernard and Mary Berenson, who bequeathed it as a research center and library to Harvard at Bernard's death in 1959. For some years I Tatti experienced growing pains as Harvard sought to define its role and raise the funds needed to restore the villa and gardens for the use of visiting scholars.

henny fired a real missile and the upshot was a memorandum to the board of overseers. Seems that only a pittance has been gathered in and that the actual use of the place has not really been spelled out.

8 DECEMBER 1961

Showed great Tiepolo painting to Ralph Lowell who was impressed. Also to Henry Shattuck who said he wouldn't give anything for the painting. This legal sage said he thought we had "enough paintings of that kind." Of course, we haven't any! Is it deep and unconscious distrust and antipathy to baroque exuberance born from Puritan antecedents? He is eighty-three or eighty-four. In any case it is utter aesthetic blindness which deserves no respect whatsoever. I admire his honesty but deplore his arrogance and patent blindness in sitting in judgement on the work of a genius. But what matter; all the staff loves the painting and I do.

14 DECEMBER 1961

Yesterday we bought the great Tiepolo *Time Ravishing Beauty*,[103] certainly one of the major works by the master in America. This was an exciting moment for me. It cost the highest sum ever paid by the museum for a work of art, namely $210,000, exceeding the Duccio[104] by $10,000. Great rejoicing amongst the staff.

---

103. Giovanni Battista Tiepolo's painting, actually titled *Time Unveiling Truth* (c. 1758), was acquired by the MFA in 1961.
104. Duccio, *Crucifixion* altarpiece, acquired by the MFA in 1945.

* * *

Dined tonight at the sisters [Aimee and Rosamond] Lamb's[105] new apartment in Berkeley St. with their cousin T. S. Eliot and his new wife Valerie as guests of honor. Very small party with Ted Ferris, rector of Trinity, as only other guest. Most pleasant evening. Mr. E[liot] has aged. Of course he is an interesting though rather professorial talker who has the unfortunate habit of addressing the floor most of the time. Much talk about the theatre. Eliot found *Becket* a disastrous play largely because it does such violence to history. But E. also stated that he had little admiration for [Jean] Anouilh in any case. Through the evening the aged groom and youngish bride were conspicuously endearing to each other, more than often holding hands and the china-doll complexioned Valerie always addressing her husband as "darling." We drove them back to Cambridge where they, for better or worse, are quartered at the Continental Hotel.

24 DECEMBER, CHRISTMAS EVE 1961

This will be the whitest of white Christmases—nine inches of fresh snow and it still falls fast. It is late: 2am and I have finished my present wrapping and labeling and I have been to midnight service at Christ Church. As always, beautiful, but the storm reduced the usual standing room only throng of worshipers. Actually I was very lucky to get home as at least two inches of snow fell after I left the house. For anthem the choir

---

105. Aimee and Rosamond Lamb inherited a collection of impressionist paintings from their parents, Mr. and Mrs. Horatio Lamb, important patrons of the MFA. Aimee (1893–1989) studied painting at the Museum School.

sang a portion of Randall Thompson's 200 Christ Church anniversary "gospel according to St. Luke." Found it movingly beautiful and even more regret not having witnessed the whole wonderful performance last week. Quite proud of my little Ford's behavior in the snow and the half-plowed streets of Cambridge, gently wallowing over the snowy ruts. Had only one moment of anxiety as I drove up Coolidge Hill. Then shoveled the driveway again having done it with Peter just two hours previous.

As always this is a moment of the year I can't bear to relinquish and I indulge my solitude, my hour alone with Christmas tree, and Christmas music. Their magic sends me back to other Christmases, the most wondrous and unforgettable day of the year and these thoughts fill me nostalgia and tearful sentiments: Greene in 1917, unbelievable amounts of snow, making our own war-time x-mas tree ornaments of paper and gilded walnut shells, popcorn and cranberry garlands; the bobsled my father named "Votes for Women"; the Humpty Dumpty circus which Santa left on the front stoop; Christmas in New Caledonia[106] and a Midnight service in the French Protestant Church; Christmas in Honolulu and the first Christmases of our children in St. Louis. Christmas in Harrisburg in 1916 with the night nurses of the neighboring hospital singing Christmas carols in the street clad in blue capes. I never hear "Joy to the World" without thinking of that magic night; and then on Christmas day Don's scenery for Wid's electric trains in the playroom in Aunt Jane's house in Front Street.[107]

---

106. Rathbone was stationed in New Caledonia from 1943 to 1945 during his service in the United States Navy.

107. Rathbone's Aunt Jane Connely, (Mrs. John) Oenslager, lived in Harrisburg and had three children—Perry's cousins Donald, Willard, and Beatrice (Mrs. Malcolm) Chace.

5 JANUARY 1962

Home from Twelfth Night party at Sarah Swetzoff's house, 50 River Street, Boston. Great throng of younger people drinking cocktails, most of them strangers, but knew Bob Gardners and Bart Hayes and half knew quite a few others. Long talk with young chap called Fassett about Karolik. Fassett undertook recording of his records of Russian songs. He marveled at how we endured Karolik from day to day, properly characterized him as a child, as insistent and egocentric. I do wonder myself and can only attribute my own endurance of this insufferable burden, this vain, repetitive, consummate, megalomaniac to well-trained patience coupled with my father's unfailing good nature, amiability, and tact. But I would really like to clobber him. He almost makes me despise my own inherent love of American Art.

13 JANUARY 1962

At 11:15 PM came back from two and a half hours alone in the Chinese exhibition. This was a marvelous experience. The exhibition is a dream of beauty, and Chinese art should only be looked at with no distractions whatsoever. First glance at the big Song hanging scrolls is always a disappointment because the silk or paper has always darkened. But looking deeper is a thrilling reward: the vitality of the brush stroke, the vocabulary of form, the individual touch of each master becomes all-absorbing. How cold and clammy the sunless chill of the winter landscapes with snow and overcast atmosphere: the Kuo Shi especially wonderful and the big Hsia Kuei hand scroll which is a Chinese "expressionist" landscape! Actually I had not seen *all* the paintings and after two and a half hours haven't seen them all yet. But now I understand better than ever the incredible enthusiasm stirred up by the show. Perhaps this is partly due to the fact Boston is steeped in a tradition of Chinese appreciation. Discovered there had been 8,045 visitors in the museum today—a record unsurpassed in a decade. Tomorrow is the last day and of course the crowds will be unfathomable.

3 FEBRUARY 1962

Felt rather old-fashioned to take the afternoon train from Trinity Place to Utica. But was happy to settle into a roomette for the six-hour ride, to doze and read without interruption— to be excommunicated from the world as in the old days when I spent twenty hours on the train between St. Louis and New York. It was wonderfully restful. In the diner sat at table with a young chap from Chicago whose son was destroyed in the hideous crash of two aircraft over Brooklyn last year. He couldn't talk about it but it was obvious why he was riding the rails.

In Utica I slept in a huge mahogany sleigh bed in the Hotel Utica. The whole room was quite old-fashioned and fitted perfectly with the train ride. The bed, marvelously comfortable. I had seen nothing like it for years and I felt far, far, from home.

New museum[108] a marvel of functional perfection. Forbidding without: it could be a tomb or cenotaph; it is nevertheless warm, livable within and surprisingly extends two floors below grade. Next door is "Fountain Elms," a marvel of Victorian

---

108. Munson-Williams-Proctor-Arts-Institute

architecture and decoration. The President, William Munning, and curator, Parmenter, showed us its wonders of richly carpeted and wallpapered rooms in the high grandiloquent style of the age, its really wonderful furniture and bric-a-brac—no Beacon Street house of the age was ever better appointed. Here for the first time I saw mahogany furniture of a quality, lamps and bric-a-brac that compares with those things I grew up with and were the domestic pride of the Rathbones and the Dederers[109] in little Greene, seventy-five miles to the South. Initially the recent director, Richard McLanathan, was mentioned. This sad specimen of a museum man, my former curator of decorative arts had expelled himself by maladministration after two years. The amiable Joe Dorato, assistant par excellence, told me that McLanathan had immediately announced upon arrival in Utica that he was supposed to be director of the Museum of Fine Arts.[110] Of course there was not a word of truth in this. But it was the same lie he had told before I came to Boston.

I completed my judging in the course of one day and pressed on to Buffalo by train. There I was carried by taxi across a snowy landscape to the country club where I arrived late for Seymour Knox's dinner for dozens of out of town guests and the chief supporters of art in this city which still seems to possess something of the frontier. Found myself next to Jane Ritchie[111] full of alcoholic warmth and talking sixteen to the dozen about all the Rockefellers you could think of. Then the

---

109. The Dederers were Rathbone's ancestors on his paternal side, descendants of Dutch merchants in New York City and upstate.

110. Richard McLanathan (1916–1998), curator of decorative arts at the MFA at the time of Rathbone's appointment, had aspired to the directorship, which led to an awkward professional relationship between them.

111. Jane Ritchie was the wife of Andrew Ritchie, then director of the Yale University Art Gallery.

grand departure and in the moving coat getting throng found myself rubbing elbows with both McLanathans—no doubt on a job hunt. Even our perfunctory greetings were full of insincerity and I was glad when they passed by.

Stayed with the David Thompsons in their hospitable house, 32 St. Catherine's Court, where the [Andrew] Ritchies[112] and Tom Howe were also guests. Of course we sat and talked and drank and even danced the twist until 4:30 am. Both the younger Thompsons at home and they added to our gaiety.

Convocation in the morning at which Herbert Read[113] spoke with humility about problems of collecting in mid-twentieth century. Followed by a Japanese architect who spoke English which sounded exactly like Japanese. After ten minutes of this Tom Howe and I withdrew and I explored new museum which is overpoweringly modern. Addition of new auditorium is most skillfully designed by [Gordon] Bunshaft of Skidmore, Owings, Merrill though in its severity and "black-glass" effect has the look of a modern tomb of importance. Within everything is glacial white—walls, ceiling, floors and outside the expanses of glass the perfect white of fresh snow. This background is flattering to certain modern works, but the Buffalo authorities have assumed that it is the perfect foil for all art. In consequence the old pictures have the pitiful effect of butterflies pinned to cotton batting. All the walls of the interior of the old Grecian style building are uniformly clinical white. Most of the galleries have been usurped by the raucous oversized paintings of the past decade and the rather choice early

---

112. Andrew Ritchie (1907–1978) was director of the Albright Art Gallery in Buffalo before it was renamed the Albright-Knox Gallery as a result of Seymour Knox's patronage.
113. Sir Herbert Read (1893–1968) was an English art historian, critic, and philosopher.

paintings of the fifteenth, eighteenth, and nineteenth centuries occupy lesser galleries equally refrigerated by white walls. Such total surrender to a modern fad seems insensitive, not to say deplorable to me. In the compulsive enthusiasm for modernity inspired by Mr. Knox, all the historical continuity which once was evident in Buffalo has been obscured. Years ago Gordon Washburn[114] established there the room of contemporary art. Today it is as if the contents, the denizens of that room, had assumed the nature of the rampaging Nemean lion and had broken violently out of bounds and possessed the entire premises. Vast canvases by C[lyfford] Still and [Alan] Davie occupy space that never would have been accorded old masters even if they had been obtainable. This is the wonder. One feels that all confidence in the collection of early works had been lost.

At the last minute I was summoned to a dinner at the Knox's where I sat next to Mrs. Knox. This was before the ball at the museum. Seymour deeply savoring the moment, extracted toast upon toast from his guests and even I finally felt called upon to utter a "from the citadel of conservatism" toasted "the frontier of modernism." Then we proceeded to the Albright (now)-Knox Gallery to dance. This affair was only lightly indulged in by my house companions who were leaving when I arrived. Home by 2am. Much hysterical fun with Ritchie and Howe in the kitchen, the former preparing himself a breakfast and unbelievably funny wrestling with the trays and other fixtures in the ice box.

---

114. Gordon Washburn (1904–1983) was director of the Albright Art Gallery from 1931 to 1942 and introduced its first gallery of contemporary art in 1939. He resigned in 1942 to become the director of the Rhode Island School of Design Museum.

16 FEBRUARY 1962

A late start but unusual day at museum. Later in the afternoon to D'Arcy Edmondson's (British consul) in Chestnut st.
for cocktails in honor of Alec Waugh[115] and a plug "inciden-
tally" for the MacDowell Colony where he is now in residence.
He's a very chipper, jolly old boy and he spoke on a "soapbox"
with humor and great aplomb about the life of a novelist and
how great a haven for his ilk the MacDowell Colony is. Almost
monastic, one would gather. Nancy G. had the Bakalars in tow,
picked up from our party, and they seemed to be enjoying the
new world which is opening to them. Of course I like to see
this and feel partly responsible. Saw the Henry Laughlins after
many months. H. was full of wonder at having seen Rettles
and me dancing the twist at the Cambridge dinner dance last
week! It's true that we were about the only ones who could!
Also talked with Adelaide Marquand[116] who announces she has
"practically" sold the house next door to us without ever moving in! And for just the price she paid, namely $80,000. Buyers
will be either Leon Kirchner, new head of music at Harvard or
the Robert Bradfords who already are neighbors—just behind
our property. A[delaide] quite dashingly attired in leopard
skins, including a hat of same.

Home and changed to tails to dine at the Murray Forbes' in
Beaver Place—a spacious domicile revamped from an old mews
but having been created in the teens or early twenties in the

---

115. Alec Waugh (1898–1981), brother of Evelyn Waugh, was a
novelist.
116. Adelaide Marquand was the second wife of John P. Marquand,
author of *The Late George Apley* and other novels that satirized Boston
society. They divorced in 1958.

Italian Renaissance—English Tudor style, a style most highly regarded by one as a boy (Westchester was full of such houses, newly fabricated) but now appearing as old-fashioned and unbelievable as high Victorian. Bostonians have a way of accepting what already exists, and the Forbes house is just that. It was a bit like occupying a stage setting. Excellent dinner at which Murray carved the turkey (no servants) and the young ladies of the family handed the plates around. The Prescott Everetts and Ben Riggs the other guests. Then to Mrs. Sohier Welch in Louisburg Square for a waltz party. Climbed to second floor to leave our coats—the thing that Dickens complained about on his visit to Boston in 1844!

The double parlor filled with waltzing couples when we arrived at about 10:30 and all the gents in tails. In the dining room beyond a limitless supply of good champagne. I suppose the scene was more like that described by George Templeton Strong in his diary over a century ago than anything still existing in the world. For there was indeed a deep Victorian flavor about the entire party. Three musicians, violin, cello, and piano sounded the music from the corner and the floor was always crowded with avid, swirling dancers reflected in the huge mirrors and lit by many candles. Waltzed with the aged and charming Mrs. Sohier Welch who created the waltz evenings[117] years ago. Though reasonably conservative in my steps with her she soon begged off with the perfect excuse that she had to "go tea hostess." Such anachronistic affairs do contribute to Boston's uniqueness. Rettles adores it and so do I.

---

117. The Rathbones were regular attendees of the Boston "Waltz Evenings," founded in the 1930s and usually held in the ballroom of the Sheraton Plaza Hotel in Copley Square.

21 FEBRUARY 1962

We have a man in space![118] Great excitement all day yesterday knew nothing of it till reaching the Museum, but word spread fast from radio listeners . . . and then the hour-long anxiety about Col. Glenn's safe landing in the ocean. For the close many gathered in the guard's smoking room downstairs to watch tv screen and listen to commentary. A little after 3 P.M. we could relax when news of Glenn's safe boarding of the destroyer *Noa* was announced. One could only feel that one's private emotion at this crucial moment was shared by millions throughout the world but especially in the U.S. And the sense of the historic moment was clearly present; perhaps the most significant in my lifetime.

Lunched at Adelaide Marquand's in Cambridge. Large party in honor of Buckminster Fuller, geodesic architect-designer. So many people had no chance to talk to him but enjoyed the good food and company of many friends: Florence Hammond, Bruce and Effie Hopper, John Bullitt, Alden McIntyre, et al. Stopped at Brattle Sq. to buy new battery for Ford and while waiting went to P.O. to buy stamped envelopes. To my amazement saw new "Project Mercury" stamps. The surprise so delighted me I bought a whole sheet, though no stamp collector. Clerk told me the stamp was a total surprise to p.o. and only released today.

---

118. On February 20, 1962, John Glenn was the first American astronaut to orbit the earth.

2 MARCH 1962

Worked till 2 A.M. on annual report so fairly tired at end of day when it was time to dress for dinner with the Charles Sumner Birds at 44 Beacon st. But with a ten-minute catnap felt restored by time cocktails were served. An ultra-Boston evening: first of all the setting, impossible anywhere but here or perhaps London. Tight against the Somerset Club to the east, it breathes the same atmosphere, well-used, quite dowdy, implacably unchanging, pretentious only in its self-satisfied air. Can't believe it has changed at all since Birds bought it years ago to prevent its demolition for a high modern apartment building. Drinks in the drawing room above, then downstairs to dinner, then up again—a Boston dinner pattern imposed by antique architecture, in this case a building of 1817. Then the company: Charlie Bird, a merry positively Dickensian type with inborn graciousness and savoir faire and the urbanity that comes from rubbing elbows with the British all his life. And Julia his wife, tall, spare, erect and a bit vague but having the way of one always used to privilege. Mrs. Schenk was there, the widow swathed in purple silk and a lively talker, and old Joe Leland the architect, deaf in one ear but a vigorous diner-out, nevertheless. Also the Guido Pereras, the long and short, he a sawed-off Latin, she a tall beauty, and both the soul of geniality; and the Henry Laughlins, he another Dickensian one and also deaf on one side. Ret was a bit disconcerted sitting between the two deaf gents. I had Julia on my left and Helen Isaacs to the right. After the gents had polished off a bottle or two of champagne we ascended to the ladies and Faith Perera sang a few light numbers most charmingly while Guido P. accompanied her on the piano that hadn't been tuned in years. Nothing could have troubled the Birds less. Julia showed me her pictures—modern French. None of much consequence except a little [Eugène] Boudin and a charming, tiny [Albert] Marquet. The real distinction is the furniture, family portraits and suites of chairs and sofas in dining room and drawing room brought from England and France by two or three generations of forbears.

23 MARCH 1962

Home from dinner at Jim Lawrence's in Brookline: the [Mason] Hammonds, Craig Wylies, Mary Harriman, young Ed Lawrence and the Contessa Carpenetto who seems to be a serious aspirant for the hand of our host. Excellent dinner by candlelight. Jim lives well amid the romantic setting he has sedulously created for himself. Sat next to the Contessa who has passed twenty-one years of life in Geneva, somewhat to her regret. This town she describes as a very pretty little hole. Switzerland is all right for those born Swiss, but not for her, born Italian. She is a portrait painter, of some talent, perhaps. Anyway, very good looking. I dislike the bleak room where we sat after dinner. It contains no pictures, only some feeble sconces and mirrors on very high walls. Jim has the rather fatuous idea that "flowers and friends" should be the decoration. The poor Contessa deplored the absence of anything interesting on the walls—a feeling I have had before. The ladies love to speculate about the Contessa and the widower Jim.

But I must revert to a week ago, Saturday night the 17th when I was in New York for the 25th anniversary dinner dance that Don and Zorka [Oenslager] gave at the Colony Club. Some three hundred guests gathered at 8 o'clock and drank cocktails

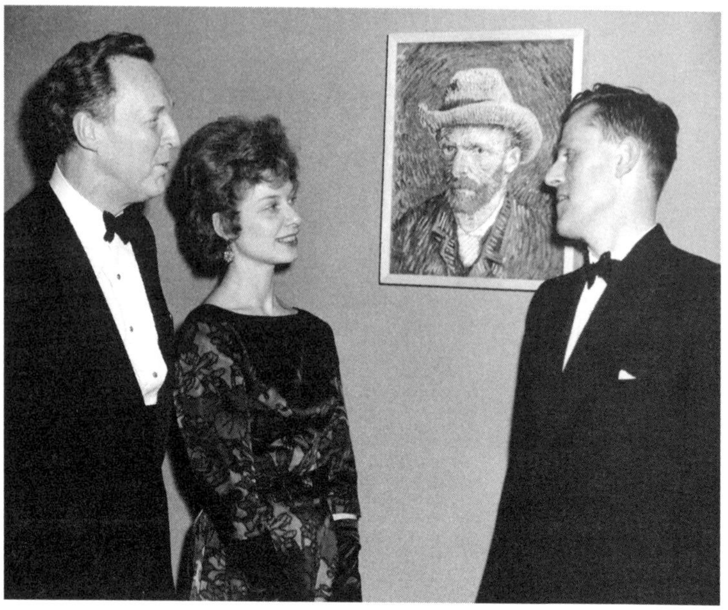

Rathbone with Mrs. and Mr. Johan Van Gogh, celebrating the opening of the Van Gogh exhibition at the MFA on March 21, 1962.

for an hour. Many strangers to me of course, but many friends. Arrived with Thornton Wilson who proves how impossible New York is for having known Donald all my life and Zorka for twenty-five years and Wilson for three years, still I didn't know they knew one another. "Have known them both for years," said Wilson. Much mingling about during cocktails and happily found myself next to Judy Winchester at table. Meyer Davis' music and champagne flowed in unison and abundance and I had a lovely time dancing with Judy and Mary Mathews, Zorka, Cassie Brown, with my cousin Jane (Chace) Clay with Jean Stralem and finally with Miriam Hopkins. All Oenslager parties have a certain zip and in spite of the very large crowd and a dense dance floor, Don and Zorka were the paddlewheels in this vortex. Ret and I have many friends but I doubt if we could bring together three hundred! The size of so personal a party, the indescribable variety of the guests, the terribly routine prosaic nature of the dinner itself made me realize how immense, how impersonal New York is compared with Boston. Rettles very much missed but her distaste for New York and her addiction to skiing[119] left no choice for her when the opportunity to stay at the Hallowells' house in Franconia with all three children presented itself.

Had spent the morning with the sister and brother-in-law of Louis Stern in his lovable red apartment at 444 East 52nd st. with Hanns [Swarzenski] and Eleanor Sayre exploring the collection and the fabulous library with a view to making a case for the inheritance of the whole thing by the MFA. An arduous assignment. Then to Veau d'Or in 60th st. for a good lunch.

Tuesday night Mr. and Mrs. Johan Van Gogh[120] for dinner. He surprisingly like his great uncle in looks. Also in behavior probably—taciturn and introspective. His lively very pretty young wife interested only in dancing and flirting after dinner. The Coxes and Hanns S. with us. A little music from the phonograph and the evening turned into a waltzing, twisting affair of which Johan was the silent observer puffing on his pipe as his wife whirled around with me in the waltz. No waltzing in the Netherlands according to her and she made the most of

---

119. Rettles was an avid skier and a former member of the British women's racing team, competing in Sun Valley, Mürren, Davos, and other ski resorts in the 1930s.
120. Johan van Gogh (1890–1978) was the artist's great nephew. His father, Vincent Willem van Gogh, was the founder of the Van Gogh Museum in Amsterdam.

her Cambridge fling. Her mother-in-law Nell had asked her to deliver a kiss to me! Of this she wanted to make sure more than once. We won't forget Anna who was once a ballet dancer, she said.

Van Gogh opening a great success. Dinner party for twenty at Somerset Club beforehand with Charlie Coolidge as host followed by reception for over six hundred at museum @ $5 each subscription. This made for an elegant, relaxed uncrowded affair with choral and instrumental music performed in the gallery above the Rotunda after the speech by Mr. Slingenberg, consul general of Netherlands from New York who represented the ambassador.

31 MARCH 1962

Van Gogh show attracting huge throngs—about fifteen thousand paid admissions already and over $8000 worth of catalogues, postcards, reproductions sold. Exhibition wonderfully exhilarating and a thing I feel impelled to look at every day. Right now we are also installing paintings in new Spanish gallery which unconventionally combine a wall of later Gothic works with Greco, Velázquez, Murillo, Zurbáran.

2 APRIL 1962

Yesterday evening Sir Kenneth Clark[121] rang up to announce his arrival. Obliquely asked to see the museum today, Monday,

---

121. Sir Kenneth Clark (1903–1983) was director of the National Gallery in London from 1934 to 1945. In 1969 he hosted the popular miniseries *Civilisation* for BBCTV.

though closed. Of course he was welcome and I invited him for lunch at the Harvard Club with Hanns [Swarzenski].

All morning with our architects talking about changes in the Asiatic department, especially India and Persian; also about new lighting scheme for modern gallery. A blessing to deal with Nat Saltonstall who readily groups ideas and is mercifully free of the vanity that grips most architects. Kay Clark appeared at noon and we kept our luncheon date. Stimulating company—a man who really looks at everything (which is rare). We gossiped happily about international art world. He had spent eleven days in California where he was enchanted by L.A. and somewhat disenchanted by San Francisco. In latter saw nothing but trustees and wanted really to see LIFE. Agreed with me that theft of Goya *Duke of Wellington* was work of English idealist outraged at such an expenditure. Horrified by predatory behavior of Sotheby's.

4 APRIL 1962

Yesterday lunched at [James] Plaut's in Cambridge for K[enneth] Clark. Twelve or fourteen guests mustered for the agreeable event—my third meal with Sir Kenneth in two days, but not my last as he readily accepted Ret's invitation to dine, or rather sup, simply with us, and early before driving out to Wellesley [College] for his lecture in the evening. Made excellent company. He's a sharp observer and a quick, rather tart, talker. Full of praise for museum which he really canvassed with great efficiency and remarkable power of absorption. He does look extraordinarily like a turtle, as Hanns observed, not only round the nose and mouth, but even in the eye. And he's a bit snappy too; even knows and admits he's been rude. Very keen about the faience in the house which he also collects. Has an admirable mind, clear and penetratingly analytical. There's a certain suppressed romanticism in his nature which peeps out occasionally. Mostly it is under control of his intellectuality. All was brilliantly deployed in his lecture which traced the development of artistic attitude resulting in current world-wide "tachism" and a prophesy of its eventual though still remote disappearance. Beautifully phrased and delivered, he spoke to big audience of about a thousand. Afterwards to Dean [Teresa] Frisch's pleasant home on the campus for a fine collection; then home with Hanns, Sir Kenneth returning with Plauts, and eventually to bed.

27 APRIL 1962

To Tufts University theatre with Ret to see Judith Anderson and Bill Rorick in scenes from *Macbeth* and a condensed version of *Medea*. The Dame's performance was magnificent; Bill's adequate. He has too much sangfroid for great tragic roles. But he has a good understated feel for his fabulous dramatic gifts. Her voice range unbelievable from a whisper to wild stentorian growls. Saw *Medea* a dozen years ago and was impressed again with the beauty of Robinson Jeffers' poetry.

Dame Judith and Bill and their traveling secretary came to us for drinks afterwards. Judith has most unpretentious manner and gracious friendliness. Bill suffering from a cold and drinking no more than honey and vinegar. Having recently been in Cleveland they informed me that museum had bought the big, mechanical and "official" [Jacques-Louis] David of *Cupid and Psyche* of the Brussels period. This is the painting Heinemann showed me a year ago and which I would not want for any money. At the same time I saw our Tiepolo for first time and it was easy for me to choose between the two. Boston has the masterpiece and Cleveland has the machine.

Van Gogh show approaching its triumphant close. Over 110,000 visitors as of this date—a record-breaking attendance in history of the museum. The exhilaration of these paintings seems to be absolutely irresistible to vast throngs of people.

V[incent] W[illem] van Gogh is here to conduct paintings and drawings back to Holland. Took him and Hanns [Swarzenski] and Rosamond Bernier (editor of *L'Oeil*) to lunch at Harvard Club.

28 APRIL 1962

Slept late and lazily. Today another summer temperature. Spent an hour after late rising fertilizing lawn and spreading some new chemical to kill crab grass. Then dressed hurriedly in light summer things to go to Lincoln with Theodora Codman to lunch with ancient Miss Dorothy Codman in really ancient Codman house[122] which will one day be condemned to blessed preservation and the rigor mortis of the Preservation Society. One deplores time's inexorable rule and sighs for the day when such noble, spacious, yes, pretentious houses, could be occupied—and happily—as a matter of course. Now, alas, they must be a public charity or disappear. The dear old house has proudly stood in its ancient meadow for two hundred years. Nothing around it suggests the crass changes of our time. I felt, as we approached, that we could just as well be in a carriage, our horse-drawn vehicle of another generation. From without one felt no encroachment of modernity. There were no signs at all.

---

122. The Codman House in Lincoln now belongs to Historic New England.

No light or power lines; no modern pavings; no modern "chic" touches. This dark gray painted house with its white trim, its pure country setting, could have greeted the eye of a pre-Revolutionary colonist. Within we were greeted by Miss Codman, pushing eighty, a perfect personification of the New England spinster, informed to the letter and proud of every detail of the house and prepared to give every generation its credit or discredit for the present states of every room. Lunched with her in dining room transformed beyond recognition into high Victorian taste. But rest of the house crowded with fine old furniture, portraits by [John Singleton] Copley and [John] Smibert and lots of faience. Also a surprising number of old Dutch pictures hiding under varnish crazed and dark. At Theodora's prodding Miss C. finally relinquished for the museum Copley's only still life painting—a trompe l'oeil of a steel corkscrew hanging on a hand-wrought nail and painted on a door in the front room to left of entrance.[123] When this woodwork was removed in the seventies this bit of the stile was salvaged and preserved. Family story is that Copley on a visit sometime before he left Boston in 1774 painted the corkscrew so the house would never be without one. Wanting to open a bottle for conviviality's sake, his host, Mr. Codman could not find a corkscrew!

25 MAY 1962

Word at last from Louvre by cable that it will lend eight Barbizon paintings. This is six more than originally agreed to by Bazin who is world's most difficult museum director. And it

---

123. *Corkscrew Hanging on a Nail* by John Singleton Copley (late 1760s) is now in the collection of the MFA.

has taken all but [President Charles] de Gaulle to obtain this loan. Even wrote to [André] Malraux,[124] talked with his right hand, [Jacques] Jaujard, our ambassador [Hervé] Alphand, our consul [Jean] Savelli; also American minister in charge of cultural affairs of New York. Even though we failed to get all fourteen loans, at least Barbizon show will have importance and prestige it deserves with Louvre loan. But *so* much to do to wind up matters before taking off.

Dinner of "the Club" at Billy Aldrich's in Brookline. Large percentage on hand. A perfect spring evening, so cocktails on terrace overlooking the lawn where great beech trees sweep the grass. Talk of Carpenter's astronomic achievement[125] and gossip about our president's former marriage—a civil one which was annulled and suppressed. So suppressed in fact that it only reached my ears when Jean Brooks came for cocktails this week. Apparently wife #1 is now happily married to someone else. Fine dinner according to old tradition. Then Billy sought to impress upon us the requirement to draw and render according to the old Beaux Arts discipline under which he was trained. His early renderings of monuments, pavilions and other useless but perhaps ornamental buildings belong to another world and to an age so remote one can't believe they are only sixty years old. Home by eleven P.M.

Eliza now begins to take note not only of her own clothes but mine too. She passes judgment on my combination of tie, shirt, and suit. Belinda even tries to ordain what I shall wear! B. is no longer a child. Suddenly and somewhat sadly there no longer are any children in the family.

---

124. Andrè Malraux (1901–1976) was France's first minister of cultural affairs, a post he held from 1958 to 1969.
125. Malcolm Scott Carpenter (1925–2013) became the second astronaut to orbit the earth—after John Glenn—on May 24, 1962.

28 MAY 1962

Yesterday was Sunday and I worked the day on Beckmann lecture, sitting at card table in the garden and writing and resisting the temptation to garden, i.e. to pull weeds. A superb May day. At 6 came Ibby Halsted[126] and Mr. Aly Khaled, curator of Alexandria Museum in Egypt. A nice obsequious man who got to his feet each time Ret and I passed something to him. Much impressed by educational and television program of museum. Spoke of brilliance of architectural solution of new museum in Turin. Intelligent man, I think, but ill at ease. Then came super-confident Richard Feigen of Chicago, young art dealer formerly stockbroker. Full of enthusiasm for Beckmann. Nice talk about popular position of Beckmann amongst modern collectors, hope of Chicago Beckmann show etc.

26 SEPTEMBER 1962

Dined tonight at the Stouts' at Fenway Court where Mrs. Higgins of Worcester was a guest and also Dr. Blumgart and wife. The guest of honor was an Indian from New Delhi who has recently been made superintendent of all restoration activities for Indian Museums. Mrs. B. had visited I Tatti in the spring and found it a wilting and spiritless institution which confirms other reports I have heard about its post-Berenson existence. Kenneth Murdock[127] and his wife struggle with the

---

126. Isabella "Ibby" Halsted (1907–2006) was secretary of the MFA's Ladies Committee and a neighbor in Cambridge.
127. Kenneth Murdock (1895–1975), Harvard professor of history and literature, was the first director of the Villa I Tatti, from 1961 to 1964.

place but it does not seem to renew itself under the Harvard dispensation and again, one questions the wisdom of the corporation in accepting the bequest. B. left $1,000,000 and Harvard has expected to raise $2,000,000 more. This has not been forthcoming. Why? As Mr. Murdock said to me at the Tavern [Club] in the spring, "People seem to be of two minds about Mr. Berenson." The truth is that Berenson has no great appeal to the un-snobbish world. He was not a dis-interested scholar. Meyer Schapiro expressed it in his review of Sylvia Sprigge's book when he said, "Business was the concealed plumbing in Berenson's house of life."

Talk with George [Stout] about the surely impending [Walter] Chrysler scandal.[128] Ralph Colin[129] on telephone in New York today said all customs agents have been alerted to seize the fraudulent works upon their return from the National Gallery of Canada to the USA. Two dealers, Alex Rosenberg and Eleanor Seidenberg have designated seventy-one absolute fakes and possibly eleven more in addition. Have not tallied my own count with theirs, but believe it would agree. Colin also said a national magazine would expose the frauds in a number to be published in midst of Canadian show of the collection. Am

---

128. In 1962, a large number of paintings in an exhibition at Walter Chrysler Jr.'s eponymous museum in Provincetown, drawn from his vast private collection, were discovered to be fakes when the show traveled to the National Gallery of Canada in Ottawa in September of that year. Though there were no direct consequences of the scandal, it was a landmark event in drawing attention to the lack of regulation in the art market.

129. Ralph Colin (1900–1985), a modern art collector and attorney, founded the Art Dealers Association of America in 1962 to codify best practices and create a reliable art appraisals system in response to threats from the IRS to abolish tax-deductible gifts of art to museums. Colin was the first to cast doubt on the authenticity of certain works in the Chrysler collection.

glad I wrote to Chrysler two weeks ago expressing my concern about certain paintings after my visit to his museum with Margaret McKean and Lily Saarinen in August.

1 OCTOBER 1962

Recommenced this diary two years ago today when I addressed Colby Junior College in New Hampshire. Is it a waste? In looking back over the preceding pages, I know how omnivorous time swallows up the detail of our lives. I am astonished at how much of this trivia I would have totally forgotten had I not written it down. I know my life is rich, but to read about it makes it seem richer than I could ever remember it to have been.

7 OCTOBER 1962

Back from Chicago via New York Friday A.M. the 5th. Occasion was opening of the new Morton [salt] wing and the vernissage of the *Treasures of Versailles Exhibition* which we had declined for reasons of insufficient quality. At Art Institute first morning was promptly buttonholed by [Harold] Joachim,[130] drawing curator who proudly showed me ravishing new acquisitions of his department, then led me on tour of renovated, rearranged and new sections of museum. Second floor of Morton wing looks like airplane hangar—vast, lofty hall (about thirty feet high) where for reasons too fanciful for logic, Jim

---

130. Harold Joachim (1909–1983) was curator of prints and drawings at the Art Institute of Chicago.

Speyer[131] has hung the modern collection as close to the floor as possible. But generally the place looks clean and inviting for first time in years.

Upon viewing Versailles show, greatly relieved not to be bringing it here. First remark made to me by Mlle. Champin, French traveling curator-in-charge put to me was, "Well, do you like it or hate it?" She was rather disparaging of it herself, and with good reason. One might say the show is "for export only." It is indeed a vast official concoction with good propaganda value for the undiscriminating. Though there were some brilliant works like David's *Marat Assassinated*[132] and his unfinished huge *Oath of the Tennis Courts*, the entire ensemble had for me the look of a sale room before a very expensive auction. In the midst of it all was Josephine's diamond tiara lent to be sure not by Versailles, but by the jewelry merchants of New York, Van Cleef and Arpels. Opening thronged by 580 dinner guests who after a noisy half hour of cocktails filed into a huge improvised banquet hall surrounded by paper hedgerows and adorned with a very showy dais and baldachin. There sat the French principals and their beauteous wives, Mme [Nicole] Alphand, especially so, with Bill Blair and Mrs. Morton at the center. [Hervé] Alphand[133] spoke well and wittily. [Gerald] Van der Kamp, curator of Versailles also spoke taking the occasion to enumerate all the generous Americans who had contributed to the shoring up and restoration of various parts of the palace. Last named was Mrs. Barbara Hutton who "had restored the King's bedroom" a citation which to Van der Kamp's surprise

---

131. A. James Speyer (1913–1986) was curator of modern art at the Art Institute of Chicago in the 1960s.
132. Jacques-Louis David's *The Death of Marat*
133. Hervé Alphand (1907–1994) was France's ambassador to the United States from 1956 to 1965.

and confusion brought down the house. I sat next to young Mrs. Brooks McCormick and a Mrs. Glove, a solid matron with little or no interest in art. Surprised to find Nate and Ann Pusey amongst the crowd and delighted that Joe and Lulu Pulitzer also turned up. After milling about for awhile went off to Susie Zurcher's apt for a late party. Then a long talk with Tom Howe and the beautiful Francesca whose nose has been quite charmingly altered (!) and Jim Foster[134] at the Drake before bed.

22 OCTOBER 1962

President Kennedy announced Cuban crisis[135] at 7 P.M. in televised address to the nation. A grim, form, uncompromising speech which made my heart beat faster with dread of the possible consequences. The awful preoccupations, the relentless tension of the war years loom again on the horizon of my imagination. Great speculation all day as the president was closeted all of Sunday with his cabinet and his advisors. The Russians now know exactly where we stand and we are closer to atomic war than ever before.

---

134. James Foster was director of the Santa Barbara Museum of Art from 1957 to 1963, and director of the Honolulu Academy of Arts from 1963 to 1982.

135. The Cuban Missile Crisis began with the Soviets' installation of nuclear missiles in Cuba, sparking a military standoff between then Soviet leader Nikita Khrushchev and President Kennedy, which ended when Khrushchev agreed to remove the missiles in exchange for Kennedy agreeing not to invade Cuba.

10 NOVEMBER 1962

A word about the St. Louis weekend 2–5 Nov. Rett and I flew out by TWA Friday P.M. arriving in time to go straight to [Richard] Weil's[136] supper party where most of our intimate friends were gathered. Felt immediately cradled in St. Louis love and hospitality. Weil's collection grows more and more up-to-the-minute. The less than up-to-the-minute works are pushed into the background: the Klees into the bathroom for instance, while the new Dubuffets occupy more honored positions in the bedroom.

Leisurely breakfast *en negligee,* then lunch party at Fran Cook's handsome house on Overhill's drive with Zeekie Pettus, the Niedringhousens, Bernoudys, [W. Julius] Polk[y] and John Harney. Afterwards to the Artists Guild to the exhibition and make notes for Sunday's events. Elegant dinner at Pulitzers' before the ball at the Halls' house. We were guests of Martha Love and Mary [Hall] and shared honors with the former orchestra conductor, [Edouard] van Remoortel and his new wife. The entire occasion could not have been more gay in the best St. Louis style and tradition. Vans had moved out all the furniture in the morning leaving hall and dining room free for dancing and plenty of space for chairs and tables decorated with floriated champagne bottles and candles and vines charmingly wandering over the walls. About eighty guests assembled and we danced to the lively strains of musicians placed on the landing of the stairs. The whole scene was a splendid and perfect concoction of Mary's romantic heart. Every able-bodied person we knew was there and we waltzed, fox-trotted, twisted

---

136. Richard and Florence Weil were avid collectors of modern art in St. Louis. Florence was the daughter of Mark and Etta Steinberg.

until nearly 3 in the morning, having arrived at 10:30. The willowy Anne Deloge Werner looked like a Lautrec poster in a sheath with flounces and a feather boa with which she entwined her partners, including me. By the time I took her as a partner I really didn't know that I was dancing! The twist was not enough for her. "Let me show you the twine," she said; and she did! The hours zipped by and I was on my way home with Rett, Bill and Gertrude [Bernoudy][137] long before I had had enough.

Pleasant Sunday morning buffet again *en negligee* with Bill. But lovely relaxation was hours away; i.e. after the performance at the museum at 4 P.M. The panel talk with [Fred] Conway and Wally Smith went off with great éclat with me as moderator sitting between the two protagonists of the show.[138] Audience of nearly four hundred seemed to like the proceedings and I wondered why I had any apprehensions at all.

Drinks with Francie Catlin and Merrill Rueppel[139] (assistant to Charles Nagel[140]) at former's house before supper party at Etta Steinberg's where she was her shy, gracious self amidst her fabulous collection. All the beautiful paintings looked more wonderful than ever.

---

137. William "Bill" Adair Bernoudy (1910–1988), an architect and protégé of Frank Lloyd Wright, designed many houses and civic buildings in his native St. Louis and beyond. His wife, Czech-born Gertrude Lenart Bernoudy, was a collector of modern art and a friend of Curt Valentin.

138. Rathbone was invited to the St. Louis Art Museum to moderate a panel of artists on trends in American painting in conjunction with an exhibition of contemporary paintings from New York art galleries.

139. Merrill Rueppel (1925–2011) was to follow Rathbone as director of the Boston MFA—beginning his tenure in 1973.

140. Charles Nagel (1899–1992) followed Rathbone as director of the St. Louis Art Museum in 1955.

17 NOVEMBER 1962

Mrs. Rockefeller III rang up in the morning to say her husband was coming to museum on Monday morning to see me and Asiatic dept. At end of day G. David Thompson[141] called from Pittsburgh to invite me to judge the arts festival exhibition of that city come May '63. G. D. T. is deeply smitten with Rockefellers, now summers in Maine, even sails a boat which he bought from David! G. D. is text book example of current American "status seeking." He has graduated from being an eccentric art collector to simply "keeping up with the Rockefellers." He has little time for Rathbone these days. Once it was weekly telephone calls from Pittsburgh. Friday's contact was first in many months. So runs the world away.

18 DECEMBER 1962

This morning arranged to call Paris on phone to talk to [Jacques] Jaujard (Malraux's right hand in Ministry of Culture) about bringing *Mona Lisa* to Boston. Had persuaded rear consul-general Jean Savelli to be with me. But placing call took one and a quarter hours and Savelli had to leave just before call came through. So tomorrow I have date at consulate to try again. A rather hopeless attempt, I fear. But one must try or forever regret it. Unofficially I know the painting will be shown at Metropolitan following National Gallery. But Savelli and I have good arguments up our sleeve for Boston.

Past weeks too busy to permit a line in this book. Fogg

---

141. George David Thompson (1899–1965) was a Pittsburgh industrialist who assembled an important collection of modern art.

Visiting dinner brought Joe and Lulu [Pulitzer] in the "Weatherbird" (*Post-Dispatch* plane) with Bill Bernoudy (to study Japanese garden) and Henry McIlhenny and Gloria Etting from Philadelphia and Ralph and Georgie Colin talking at length about the scandal of Alfred Frankfurter whose U. of Berlin degree seems to be his own invention. Adelaide Marquand indulged a little too freely so Gardner Cox[142] and I saw her home and had to break into her mansion as she had left her handbag with key at our house.

Took Bill to see the monstrous new building next to the Fogg called the Carpenter Center (Harvard only builds "centers" today) which destroys the unity of Quincy St. having no relationship whatsoever to its surroundings. Nor has this tortured pile of concrete designed by Corbusier any apparent logic within or without. At present there seems to be no clear idea of the building's function and there is difficulty in finding the right director for the "center."

Bill with us till Tuesday morning after a convivial evening at the Swarzenskis following the Fogg dinner at the museum. Then in P.M. met Peggy Guggenheim at the airport and brought her home as a houseguest for three days. She couldn't get enough of the museum, found it fabulous etc. Dinner party for her with Henry Laughlins, Stouts, Joe Upton and Baldwins came for a drink beforehand. Next evening had Jan and Yvonne Cox, Hanns and Brigitte, a very happy evening. Then I was off to New York leaving Peggy for another Boston day.

---

142. Gardner Cox (1906–1988) was a well-known portrait painter who lived in Cambridge.

19 DECEMBER 1962

Dress rehearsal of Tavern [Club] Play.[143] All the family for dinner at the club and the performance. Belinda displayed her decisive critical sense by telling me precisely where the performance was weak and how it could be improved. Peter was again caught up in the spirit of it and made color flash photos of the performance. Afterwards Peter and I joined the Willises and the Hugh Shepleys at the Red Garter—a new style simple night club featuring banjo players on Warrenton St.

This morning kept my date with French consul Savelli at the consulate and talked on the phone with office of ministry of culture in Paris about *Mona Lisa*. Jacques Jaujard ill, but spoke to his assistant Charpentier. Seems to be no hope of bringing the *Gioconda*[144] to Boston, but at least the effort has been made, all arguments put forward. Without having made the effort I could only reproach myself. Now we can relax.

At the Fogg Visiting Committee meeting Mrs. Robert Woods Bliss[145] well up in her eighties felt moved to speak about I Tatti and Harvard's failure thus far to raise the necessary funds to maintain it, not only in the manner to which it was accustomed, but to make it the "center" for humanistic studies

---

143. As a member of the Tavern Club, Rathbone was occasionally recruited to the cast of the members' amateur theatricals.

144. Another name for the *Mona Lisa*

145. Robert Woods Bliss (1875–1962), a career diplomat, and his wife, Mildred Barnes Bliss (1879–1969), were art collectors who bequeathed their house, gardens, and collections that comprised Dumbarton Oaks—their home in Georgetown, DC—to Harvard in 1940. Like Berenson's vision for I Tatti, they aimed to create a museum and a center for scholarly studies. The Blisses and the Berensons were friends.

that has been envisioned. If the money is not raised, what is the alternative, she asked. It reminded her of a recent story of the aging Senator Greene of Rhode Island. On his ninety-first birthday reception a bustling dowager said to him, "Sen. B. how does it feel to be ninety-one years old?" The senator replied, "Well, considering the alternatives, not bad!"

28 DECEMBER 1962

It's 1 A.M. and we're just home from dining with Catherine Coolidge at Magnolia. A long drive for dinner but rewarding. The five first presidents by Gilbert Stuart now greet one upon entering in a little "Tempietto" entrance hall. They used to hang more conventionally on the walls of the large dining room in Brookline. Since I saw them last they have spent a five-month "holiday" at the White House as Jackie's "guests." The last time we dined with the Coolidges we used the Jefferson Chinese export porcelain dinner service. Not tonight. Guests included the Henry Cabot Lodges, Kelly Andersons, Hyde Cox, the [Robert B.] Choates of [*Boston*] *Herald*. Seated next to Mrs. Choate at dinner she complained bitterly about lack of response from state of Maryland to her proffered gift of a desk from Senate chamber of old capital at Annapolis. I assured her there would be no indifference on part of MFA!

9 JANUARY 1963

Peter has the flattering habit of coming into my study to visit late in the evening. (He's an inveterate night owl). This is very pleasant but it certainly curtails the entries in this book. Not a word as yet about Christmas—New Year. The former was true to type: stockings on our bed at 8 A.M.—like the English our children are terribly conservative and refuse to give up old habits. Any deviation from our Xmas program is sternly rejected. So stockings as usual even though the old magic of such trivial surprises has decidedly faded. Be[linda] and I trimmed the tree Xmas eve—a lovely spreading specimen, high as the room is high as usual. Every ornament and novelty coming out of the boxes delighted Bee and receives her critical appraisal. So the tree was a bright gay and glittering beauty Xmas morning sheltering an unbelievable array of boxes and packages. So the entire morning was devoted to the rite and the clean-up and preparation of the table was scarcely completed by the time our traditional and beloved guests arrived for dinner at 2. Then more presents exchanged and a long feast with the Coxes[146] and Swarzenskis. Late in the day the Vermeules came and we listened to the *First Family*[147] record—often hysterically funny. Then as usual we broke into the dance—polkas, waltzes, twists, charlestons—even the Greek handkerchief dance (simplified version). Till after midnight we rejoiced ourselves in this fashion. What dancers all of us are—even Hanns who attempts only his own free style. Bee is game to try anything now, Eliza has a good style and following ability for fourteen years, and Peter begins to show that he's "got rhythm" too! This pleases us all because it goes with his charm and sense of fun.

---

146. Jan Cox (1919–1980), a Belgian artist, taught at the School of the Museum of Fine Arts. With his wife, Yvonne, also an artist, they were close family friends and regular guests on feast days at Coolidge Hill.

147. *The First Family* was a parody recording of the Kennedy White House, starring Vaughn Meader as JFK, produced in 1962.

13 JANUARY 1963

A rainy and icy day, so treacherous for driving, in fact, that after skidding around Coolidge Hill, the girls and I made our way back in the Ford deciding not to risk getting to church. The trees in the garden are a miracle of beauty clad in ice and every dried seed pod has become a winter blossom. Rather a lazy day of reading and music and helping Eliza with her history.

Yesterday Rett and Eliza to Farmington[148] for second interview with Mrs. [Hollis] French[149] hoping to compensate for interview inadvertently omitted last November. They reported a pleasant lunch with Headmistress and warm reception indicating Eliza will be admitted next fall if any opening at all develops. Then a hurried look at Ethel Walker School at nearby Simsbury before treacherous drive home in freezing rain.

After dinner took girls to Dr. Nauen's[150] house for Brahms quintet performance where Virginia Ripley's[151] fiancé played the violin. Slow starting, of course, but lateness of hour didn't trouble Bee who had her nose as close to the keyboard as possible. She *is* musical, enjoys her lessons and loves to be coached by Ginny who plays very well. Home at a crawl over icy streets.

Friday noon drove down to Sharon with Dus Cavallo to lunch with Mrs. Henry Kendall and son and to see her collections.[152] Who would expect to find in this remote location a

---

148. Miss Porter's School in Farmington, Connecticut
149. Headmistress of Miss Porter's
150. Dr. Alice Nauen, a Cambridge pediatrician
151. Virginia Ripley was an au pair.
152. Henry (1878–1959) and Evelyn Kendall (1893–1979) were best known for their collection of whaling pictures and artifacts, the extent of which prompted them to create a museum near their home in Sharon, Massachusetts. Much of the Kendall painting collection

doll's house, and by that I mean a separate house inhabited by dolls—scores of them, all dating before 1870 and many from the eighteenth century. But one can expect almost anything to turn up in this remarkable part of the world. This is no ordinary collection but a distinguished one scrupulously cared for. Case upon case of dolls of all sizes and decades look out through their glass doors, each one perfect of its kind. And added to this are fabulous dolls' houses and dolls' stores, some created by Mrs. K. and her family, others dating in their entirety from the early nineteenth century. Mrs. K has also collected prints, paintings and fabrics relating to ballooning—hundreds of them! Fortunately we had a substantial lunch for after two hours amidst the dolls and the balloons we were immersed in the third collecting passion of the family—whaling. The latter occupies a museum by itself even more remote. Thither we drove in two cars and there saw the finest assemblage of its kind that exists: paintings, prints, scrimshaw, decorated glass and crockery, a fully equipped whaling boat and whale oil frying vats and implements, and certainly the most beautiful whale ship figurines I have ever seen.

14 JANUARY 1963

Rett felt a bit dizzy this morning and even came back to bed before I got up, having made breakfast for E. and B. . . . But she felt strong enough to dress and dine with Agnes Mongan[153]. . . before Andrew Wyeth opening at the Fogg. This is the second

has since been absorbed by the New Bedford Whaling Museum.

153. Agnes Mongan (1905–1996), a graduate of Paul Sachs' museum course, was curator of drawings at the Fogg Art Museum, Harvard, and its first woman director, serving from 1969 to 1971.

Wyeth show in Cambridge in two years. He is the modern darling of all circles—as Sargent was in his day. But he has more to say and in a technique as brilliant (tho' very different) as Sargent's ever was.

Happily here the accent was on drawings and they are marvels of draftsmanship and sensitivity of observation. However objective the reference, all his work seems to be underlaid with a poetic impulse which rescues his work from illustration and raises it to a level of broad meaning. His work is full of love of the subject and love of execution . . . but it is motivated by love of the meaning he hopes to convey. One is struck by his solitary and single minded absorption. He is a master of light—and of the peculiar hard, even harsh light of North America, rarely captured by his countrymen. I enjoy his art and respect him profoundly for his integrity—his independence. Andy was there, receiving in line with the [John] Coolidges, Agnes M[ongan], Phil Hofer. Then we found ourselves in a throng of people, most of whom we know. The Fogg really caters to the carriage trade! There were David and Peggy Rockefeller, Catherine Coolidge and Hyde Cox, Betty Angel from New York and Coe Kerr from Knoedler's. The close air soon gave Rettles a sinking feeling and we came home early.

17 JANUARY 1963

Home by midnight from dinner at the Dudley Pickmans'. Ted Rousseau[154] of the Met has been here two days and we are quite exhausted from attending parties for him—one of them our own. I really enjoy going to the Pickmans'. The house itself

---

154. Theodore Rousseau (1912–1973) was a controversial curator of paintings at the Metropolitan Museum for nearly thirty years.

fascinates me.[155] A dark, cavernous interior with lofty ceilings and a beautiful staircase with a gentle early rise so that one fairly glides to the second floor and with a feeling of nonchalant dignity. There the ceilings seem to rise even higher and the rooms have a glorious spaciousness. Tapestries, leather-bound books, flowers, dark walls and woodwork, a serpentine mantelpiece and a fire in the hearth. The substantial velvet covered furniture invites one to accept the luxury of total comfort and once seated to explore the tabletops loaded with objects. There Mrs. Shaw McKean, still charming, telling me of an old friend, a grandmother who is asked by her granddaughter when one stops thinking about love and sex, and her answer was "why do you ask me, I'm only eighty-four and I think about it every day!"

And there is Ceeci [sic],[156] the glamorous one, sitting next to me at table and fascinating me with her artificial look and natural behavior; her platinum blond hair and smooth skin and her complaints about Winston going to Brazil for three days ("he has to keep moving") and her languid indifference to all the luxury that surrounds her. Like so many of the rich I have known, she seems almost to hate it. Meanwhile I am relishing the squab to the last bone and the wines which stumbled over each other in profusion. Then to my right the mother,[157]

---

155. The forty-room Pickman house at 303 Commonwealth Avenue was designed by Stanford White and was the scene of many extravagant parties. Dudley died in 1964 and his wife, Vivian, in 1965. Soon afterward the house ended its life as a single-family dwelling.

156. "Ceezee" or C. Z. (Mrs. Winston) Guest (1920–2003) was the daughter of Vivian Pickman by her former marriage to Alexander Cochrane. A New York fashion leader, horsewoman, and socialite, she was one of Truman Capote's "Swans" and was featured in a *TIME* magazine cover story on American society on July 20, 1962.

157. Vivian Wessell (1894–1965) was an actress and singer before she

the incredible mother whose vulgarity I enjoy, her harsh voice and belly laugh, and whose appearance I can scarcely believe true: white hair standing out straight from her ears, no neck and plump bosom. One feels that this woman's role has been always to give license and freedom to all the animal appetites, and I suppose one of the reasons I like her is that I realize her potential ability to rid me of all repressions and indulge in barracks room bareness yet retain a feeling of moral and intellectual superiority. Aristocratic old Dudley, now seventy-seven, had passive but strong influence on the gent's table talk spiced by Alec Williams' wit and general sassiness. A Dr. Jones and wife present. Ted Rousseau is such a case of self-study and self-conscious refinement that he never never loses himself. Pity because he has the makings of a real live person.

A return visit to the Fogg to see Wyeths. Must somewhat revise enthusiastic appraisal of first night: too many pictures come dangerously close to illustrations to give them all the universal meaning which is their intention.

25 JANUARY 1963

Back from New York at 11 A.M. on Eastern Airlines shuttle flight. This is Friday and had left on midnight train Monday after wonderful performance of Peter Ustinov's *Photo Finish* at the Colonial as guests of Swarzenskis. Both Ret and I had seen this brilliant play in London last summer and it gains by second seeing.

New York trip begins to be a more and more familiar pattern—visits to more and more dealers to see fewer and fewer

---

married her first husband, Alexander Cochrane, with whom she had five children.

desirable pictures, sculptures, or anything else, and a more assiduous pursuit of our best collector-benefactor contacts. So with Hanns lunched with Thornton Wilson[158] and cocktails with Mrs. Pflueger who with I. G. Forbes husband is important collector of German porcelain and faience: really exquisite stuff. Cocktails at Jane [Sabersky]'s new apartment in 87th St. and dinner at the Provencal. Also a last visit to Dana Pond's studio apt to arrange sale of hundreds of his paintings, a great preponderance of these nudes. The irony of the MFA having consciously or unconsciously shunned the nude in the paintings collection to inherit hundreds of them!

An irresistible invitation to dine with Francis Robinson[159] at the Lotus Club at a "State Dinner" in honor of Joan Sutherland, certainly the greatest living coloratura. So in the borrowed dinner jacket found myself chatting with the great lady at cocktails before the dinner on the 24th. She's a tall Australian lassie without pretense of affectation, direct and friendly. But what an amazing sight she was! Her long face framed by a fantastic coiffure, Titian red hair rising in a high smooth pompadour from her forehead and swinging out to the sides like sails full of wind. Her big sympathetic eyes, dabbed with kohl, help to distract the attention from her lantern jaw. Not pretty but good looking and in her accent just a whisper of the old Australian. I had her quite to myself for a while and felt very privileged. I urged her to come to the museum, of course, when she sings in Boston for the first time in February.

---

158. Thornton Wilson was a collector of ceramics who gave generously to the Metropolitan Museum in New York and to the Boston MFA.
159. Francis Robinson (1910–1980) was the general manager of the Metropolitan Opera.

14 MARCH 1963

Now behind me are the Barbizon opening and my annual lecture for the class of the Museum, one last night, the other this morning, so I have a moment to write.

A week ago Sunday, the 10th, dinner here in the evening for Alf[red] Hentzen visiting from Hamburg, Hanns S[warzenski] (Brigitte still in Vienna) and Burgess Meredith.[160] Of course "Buz" Meredith had trouble finding the house and was a bit late, but no matter, it was a gay party and Ret cooked a magnificent paella full of everything. Afterwards John Huston the movie director came, and his friend Anne van der Hilde and Anthony Veiller, all part of the Otto Preminger company at work on the new film *The Cardinal*. B. M. stimulating and provocative as usual and really quite a "haustier," small with unkempt hair like a fox terrier, and eating nothing to speak of. Huston has a fascinating alert face, long with big gentle eyes, quick smile and agreeable voice, tall and lean and clad in Irish tweeds. All the art interested him, and Meredith too. We could have talked all night, but by 1 A.M. it was time to be serious about the night train to N.Y. so off to South Station with Alf and Hanns with enough whiskey under our belts to nullify the rock and roll, the bumps and grinds of the New Haven "Owl."

Busy days in New York. Spent first night at Chris Allen's apt; he just back from Italy and London and full of theater and open gossip. Lunched with Quappi Beckmann, Peter Selz[161]

---

160. Burgess Meredith (1907–1997), well-known actor of stage and screen, was in Boston to film *The Cardinal*.

161. Peter Selz (1919–2019) was curator of painting and sculpture at the Museum of Modern Art and co-curator with Rathbone and Harold Joachim of the Max Beckmann retrospective in 1964.

and Alf Hentzen to talk about Beckmann exhibition for New York, Boston, and Chicago. Dined at guest house of Museum of Modern Art before opening of big [Emil] Nolde show which was rather awful, full of New York types and overcrowded even though it was the pre-preview. With Hanns had cocktails with [Edward] Pfluegers who are collectors of German faience and porcelains and dined with [Bernard] Pincuses in Greenwich Village. Then fleeing from their overheated and airless penthouse, taxied far up Park Ave. to the Victor Ganzes'[162] for a night cap and a view of their Picassos. Found their attractive apartment literally plastered with the matter: scores of brilliant prints and numerous fine paintings and the Ganzes very genial hosts. Jane [Sabersky] was there and thus we had a happy close to the evening. Next two nights chez Francis Robinson. Wednesday evening to *Fidelio* at the Met and heard [Birgit] Nilsson sing. Stirring moments and wonderful singing, but the opera doesn't charm me and is deficient in arias.

19 APRIL 1963

Paid a return visit to Rosenberg and Stiebel to see for second time the fabulous master of St. Hippolytus altarpiece[163] which came to light only last year at a Paris auction. Screwed up my courage and asked the price—$450,000! But I really thought it would be more. The painting has me really bewitched and I'm convinced we really must have it for Boston! It has great visual

---

162. Victor (1913–1987) and Sally Ganz collected Picasso in depth before turning in the 1960s to contemporary American artists such as Robert Rauschenberg, Jasper Johns, and Eva Hesse.
163. *Martyrdom of Saint Hippolytus* (Flemish, fifteenth century, unknown artist) was acquired later that year by the MFA.

excitement, is of utmost rarity, extraordinary surface preservation, glowing jewel colors. And nothing is more needed than
an important early Flemish painting to complement the Roger
v[an]. d[er]. w[eyden]. in our collection. But the HOW! Cannot
stop thinking about this masterwork!

16 MAY 1963

A day of days for the Museum. Today the trustees voted
to buy one of its greatest treasures: *The Martyrdom of St.
Hippolytus* by an unknown Netherlandish master for the highest
price ever paid by the MFA for a work of art—$396,000. This
great painting—certainly the most wonderful work on the art
market—was sold at auction in Paris one year ago. At the time
I never thought it would be within our ken—too precious, too
costly. Asking price from Rosenberg and Stiebel was $450,000.
After last week's committee meeting, by telephone calls to
Rosenberg, I got price down to $396,000 which I consider not
too expensive for such a painting. Learned that the National
Gallery was after the picture but failed in effort to hold painting
by virtue of the fact that John Walker and a trustee did not
keep their date with Rosenberg and Stiebel! So we have made
a giant stride and I am thrilled to lead the museum to this new
level of excellence.

Dearest Rett,

We[164] have done the Holy Mountain and the pilgrims have
resumed with some relief the luxurious life of the Dodona.
Needless to say, it has been a perfectly fascinating experience.
We have visited six monasteries (besides the capital, Karyes)
and slept at two of them. We have spent many liturgical hours
and we have been blessed by the patriarch of Constantinople.
We have experienced the life of denial and austerity amidst
dilapidation on a grand scale, and we have tasted the comforts
of monastic life. We have been surrounded by [illegible] quiet
and sweet peace, by majestic natural beauty. We have literally
been in the Middle Ages. I have tried to write all this down in
a diary, so I will have to eliminate details in this letter. There
is just *too* much to say! The monks have been hospitality itself,
but for communication we would have been lost without Theo
[Roubanis][165]. Very few monks speak anything but Greek, and
they do love to converse with lay creatures from the modern
world. They have opened their libraries and their treasuries
full of things of great age and beauty and rarity. Yesterday we
cruised around the tip of Athos and through our binoculars
we "visited" scores of anchorite habitations, crazy little huts
and shacks clinging to steep sheer rock totally devoid of any
visible access. We disembarked at Kafsokalyvia, a colony of
artists situated on a precipice, which had immense charm

---

164. Rathbone traveled to Mount Athos with Henry McIlhenny,
Hanns Swarzenski, and Theo Roubanis. No females—human or animal—are permitted on the island.
165. Theo Roubanis was a Greek film actor.

and considerable comfort. The monks loved our visit and beckoned us ashore with waving flags and waved us away till we were out of sight. We returned to the anchorage at Daphni just in time to be the only witnesses of the grand disembarkation of the Patriarch himself, arriving for the millennial celebrations. Concourse of black-gowned clergy were put ashore in tenders from a Greek navy destroyer—escort and at last the Patriarch appeared—flowing white beard, jeweled pendant on breast, staff in hand—a figure of immense dignity, and just before he descended the ladder to the captain's gig, he waved to us, then made the cross sign in the air, and we waved back merrily. The ship was dressed with pendants and his ensign was hauled down from the main mast. As soon as he landed the ship's cannon let go with a twenty-one gun salute that scared the daylights out of us. We spent the night on the mooring and this morning visited two more monasteries on the south coast, Gregorian and Dionysiou.

23 OCTOBER 1963

Today Prince Umberto, former King of Italy came to the museum. He is a tall, trim, and debonair chap, quite affable and eager, not without knowledge, but obviously quite unprepared for what he was going to see. A dilettante without advisors. Arriving a half hour late with a couple of Roman noblemen and policemen as his entourage and led by ex. Gov. [John] Volpe, he spent a scant fifty minutes with me as escort and finally got to the print department where he waited to see engraved portraits of members of the house of Savoia. All through the painting department the pictures drew sighs of wonder and admiration from his Highness; but for the most part I could not tell whether it was the pictures themselves that moved him or his wonder at finding them in Boston. But it was all too fleeting and therefore unsatisfactory from my point of view. What irritated me was that he was going next day to visit a macaroni factory in Lawrence, an excursion that would take at least three hours. This was arranged for at the dinner tendered by Volpe where the prince was exposed to the macaroni king who, I daresay, was a political supporter of Volpe. It's easy for the politician to put macaroni before art. But the prince was willful enough in the museum and easily wandered from the path I had prepared. Why he could not have resisted the macaroni invitation, by the same token, I fail to understand. I detected that the Italian galleries made him genuinely nostalgic, and he sighed for the land from which he is exiled.

In the evening to dine with Sally Sedgwick in Beacon St before the consul-general's reception for Sir David and Lady Ormsby-Gore, British ambassador in Chestnut St on the hill. W. G. and Olivia Constable, the Bemises, Joe Coletti and Alden McIntyre at table. W. G. was characteristically artificial in never mentioning the museum in spite of current activity which has all of Boston talking, not to mention the great new acquisition of the Hippolytus altarpiece which should excite anyone interested in pictures. But I could also see that his self-conscious attitude of indifference made him quite unhappy.

19 NOVEMBER 1963

Fogg visiting weekend is over. Our house-guests, Bill and Gertrude Bernoudy left us this morning to fly back to St. Louis with Joe and Lulu Pulitzer in the *Post Dispatch* plane. Already we feel deprived of their company and their presence. All day at museum occupied with problems and projects which meant seeing people almost without interruption. Bob Hecht[166] and Bob Baldwin in A.M. settling the matter of his relationship as dealer with the MFA—the retired Yankee banker and the credit-seeking antique art sleuth from whom we have acquired many works of great merit in the four years past. Should the museum indirectly support his speculations? This was the difficult question. Anyway, an amicable and constructive meeting.

Peter Nathan came from Zurich with photographs and paintings for sale. He has a Juan Gris for $135,000, a Picasso collage for $90,000, a Monet for more than $200,000! Said our de Staël bought in '57 for $10,000 is now worth $100,000.

Yesterday was Fogg visiting all day. Principal topics were criticism of the management and present "image" of "I Tatti" and the Fogg's need for funds for purchases. Each dept spokesman in the evening voiced the same complaint. The need and justification for expansion of the collection would seem more viable if the Fogg buildings were not forever hampered by the new Corbusier building which has been reared beside it. The Fogg and Harvard have permitted this to happen. Thereby an important part of the potential for expanding the Fogg collections has been tragically frustrated in my opinion. Much of the Com[mittee] (including myself) had their first view of the "Carpenter Center." The misfortune of this building has been compounded within: it is both confusing and forbidding.

---

166. Robert E. Hecht (1919–2012) was an American antiquities dealer with a roster of major museum clients in the 1960s and 1970s. Besides selling a number of important pieces to the MFA, he brokered the sale of the Euphronios krater to the Metropolitan Museum. In 2005 he went on trial for illegal trafficking in antiquities but was never convicted.

25 NOVEMBER 1963

They buried the president today . . . and still the unspeakable tragedy seems unreal to me. The incredulity of the first moment of the news remains. And as I watched the endless solemn parade on the museum television, I felt I was watching some historical event long past or an invented spectacle. I could scarcely believe that it was now! But I think the nation feels this way. That this youthful, vibrant, much-loved man, that this idealistic leader of the free world could be destroyed in an instant without the slightest warning has so shocked and stunned us that we can scarcely accept the reality of it. And that the massive funeral could be taking place with the world's leaders in attendance four days after the exuberant welcome in Dallas is scarcely to be believed. Likewise the bizarre events that took place in Dallas after the assassination are scarcely credible. The snake who committed the crime has escaped his rightful penalty and the night-club operator has deprived us all of the unfolding of the aftermath. Of the living no one today commands such reverential respect as Jacqueline Kennedy. The pride of her bearing, her composure under her crushing burden was nobility itself. Last night I wrote her a personal letter and felt utterly inadequate in doing so.

29 NOVEMBER 1963

A wonderful letter from Jim Ede[167] today on the subject of the assassination. The impact on the British has been unprecedented. No King or Queen has brought forth such response. Feel I must send the letter to Mrs. Kennedy. Why do we feel so much for this man? It is largely because to a degree unexpected we identified ourselves with him and his young family. He genuinely admired, respected and protected with his influence and example those values in life that mean most to the cultivated, Christian idealist. This cannot be said for many presidents of the U.S. whatever else their virtues might have been. And it was his youth that gave further prestige to his outlook and genuine convictions. And now this reign of balanced, enlightened goodness is suddenly at an end. Mr. Johnson may well prove a worthy successor as statesman and politician in a troubled world. But from this Texan we cannot expect any advancement of the cultural climate of the country. But what Kennedy and his wife have begun will not be forgotten and in time there will be pressure to continue it.

---

167. Jim Ede (1895–1990), British writer, collector, and friend to artists, met Rathbone while on a lecture tour of the United States during World War II with his wife, Helen. They formed a close friendship and maintained a correspondence over the next forty years. In 1956 the Edes moved to Cambridge, England, and made four derelict cottages into what is now known as Kettle's Yard, a center for modern British art.

21 JANUARY 1964

Have just said goodnight to a group we have long hoped to entertain: Charlie Birds, Bruce Hoppers, Edmund Tafts, John Bullards amongst the older generation and the Kenneth Isaacs, for a long, long time. To all of them we are indebted for too long. We have rarely entertained such a large number without a visiting fireman. This was a party without occasion and for friends only. Really a great success. I suppose that I have an incurable taste for the appearance of affluence and security— especially if the same is rooted in the past. So with this staid group of older friends, I was especially pleased at the table to observe the ensemble, a rarer and rarer phenomenon, of old silver and linen and furniture, the symbols of the good life of America, reaching back to the end of the eighteenth century of the Rathbones and Betts and Dederers,[168] the Doughertys and the Kirkbrides,[169] who with any sense of love and respect for what has been loved, who with any sense of certainty in the age of discontinuity and change, could fail to feel as I do. Rettles concocted a wonderful Beef Romana and our guests enjoyed the Côte Rôtie Burgundy 1959.

On Sunday last, the 19th, attended the great requiem mass of Mozart in memory of the President in the Cathedral of the Holy Cross. Rett not invited because of space restrictions, but a pity because there was room beside me in pew #50, as it turned out. Found myself directly in front of Ralph and Charlotte Lowell and next to the center aisle, and to my right was O'Connor, author of *The Last Hurrah*. Arrived just in time to find myself in the cathedral vestibule while Jacqueline and Kennedy family

---

168. Family names on Rathbone's side
169. Family names on Rettles de Cosson Rathbone's side

with Eminence Cushing swathed in yards of red taffeta and ermine were being photographed and televised unmercifully. Jacqueline never flinched but almost automaton-like showed no emotion or impatience. Mixed feelings; was this the beginning of a great show-piece for the church or was this a solemn religious dedication? Can only say that this and all the rest never seemed very religious to me. Was it the setting, the personnel, or the Latin rite that destroyed the beauty and seriousness of the Holy Communion that followed? All the sublimity came from the music: chorus and orchestra under [Erich] Leinsdorf.[170] But the glorious music and the liturgy never seemed in perfect harmony to me. If only the text of the prayer book of England could have been uttered by the right voice—for all to hear and understand, accompanied and reinforced by Mozart's divine invention of sound then, oh! Then we would have had a service to make us want to kneel instead of obeying mechanically the gestures of some functionary in the sanctuary. Of course the setting was far from satisfactory. Within, the cathedral of the holy cross is an unmitigated pile of plaster in the worst style of imitation gothic concocted in the 1870s or so. One . . . is painfully conscious of highly varnished pews of "mail-order" design, of a pavement of Armstrong's linoleum.

31 JANUARY 1964

Rett drove off this noon to the mountains of Vermont for a weekend of skiing with Bee and to meet Kate Davis Quesada

---

170. Erich Leinsdorf (1912–1993) was conductor of the Boston Symphony Orchestra from 1962 to 1969.

and Ricky[171]. So alone for dinner and then to the Institute[172] in Newbury st for opening of Ellsworth Kelly exhibition. Nice talk with the beautiful Lee Gardner who like me had commenced the day attending a hearing at the State House on proposed widening of Memorial Drive.[173] The Highwaymen have determined to butcher the Charles River Parkway and transform it into a super-highway, sacrificing into the bargain the glorious stand of sycamore which border the present road and which is one of the perennial joys of Cambridge. Americans in the middle of the twentieth century live at the mercy of highway engineers and "traffic experts."

Mr. Kelly was spread around us in a vast and empty way: huge canvases of bright smooth color, simple patterns and hard edges. No one seemed to be moved or very enthusiastic, but just to be there was a ritual that had to be and had to be accepted. For now it must be recognized that those with a certain eye, a certain level of education and sophistication must at least pay lip service to modern art or be considered beyond the pale. As for me, faced with these vast canvases, I am more at sea than ever over how to formulate a policy of acquisition in the field of modern art for a great museum of historical art like the MFA.

The Greek earring[174] may be recovered and now we live from day to day, almost from hour to hour in a miasma of desperation and hope. As the truth of its theft arises to the

---

171. Kate Davis Quesada was sister of Joseph Pulitzer III; Ricky was her son.

172. The Institute of Contemporary Art was then housed on Newbury Street in Boston.

173. In 1964 a Citizen's Emergency Committee was formed and succeeded in defeating the proposal to widen Memorial Drive in Cambridge.

174. The Greek earring, a gold 350–325 BCE sculpture of a winged charioteer, was stolen from its display case at the MFA in 1964.

surface from the depths of human misery and disorder, the whole confused story is scarcely credible. It forces into our reluctant comprehension such a tangle of human depravity and vice including dope addiction, treachery and lies, brutality and masochism and even self-castration that in the resulting bewilderment over human behavior, one admits the incapacity to deal with the problem, and almost, but not quite, defeat. Cornelius and Emily Vermeule have kept on top of developments in a conscientious, emotional way that is admirable and touching. Tonight they are standing separate "watches" at home close to the phone, awaiting developments. The self-confessed thief is a psychopath whose statement to his doctor last Tuesday led to the recovery of the little Millet still-life stolen ten days earlier. But his statements regarding the whereabouts of the earring led to no easy recovery, but to conflicting evidence from his associates including the proprietor of a Cambridge dress shop, Mrs. Suki Brown. The acknowledged thief, Tom Gezork, has been Mrs. B.'s lover, but also the paramour of a model at the Museum School who now is great with his child. In remorse over this, last 22nd of December he castrated himself. But to confuse matters, he now accuses a friend of doing same. Same friend, one Bradley, he also accuses of having the earring. Separating truth from fiction and thereby finding the earring is the great burning problem of the hour.

1 FEBRUARY 1964

Working at home alone, was surprised by a telephone call from a stranger named Pat Schaffer who wanted to talk to me about the earring. Said Schaffer appeared at the house about one hour later in a bright red sports car. Young (about twenty-five years), ambitious, self-possessed, he professed his desire to help as volunteer eavesdropper, stooge, or whatever. Just out of hospital, he spent the early morning hours at a "beatnik" party in the South End and overheard conversation about theft of the earring. Not able to add much to what we know, he at least verified the facts in hand and offered the conviction that Bradley (George?) knew everything and that he had the earring in his possession. But he confessed it was the theft of the Millet that really stirred his imagination. He believes Suki Brown to be entirely innocent and that Bradley is a sort of "fence" who hopes to market the earring. He struck me as being a bit strange himself notwithstanding the fact he was running for state representative of his home district, Gloucester. A friend of friends of the circle of the thief and his woman living in beatnik style on the South End, he was able to learn a lot without showing his hand. Offering his aid he finally agreed to talk to a policeman about the case. Just then Giampaolo, the special cop assigned to the case, rang me up and I arranged an interview between them forthwith. More waiting, more patience.

28 FEBRUARY 1964

My newest Harvard peeve was brought on repeatedly when Rett and I went to Elmwood[175] for cocktails with the new denizens of that ancient and beloved mansion. These are very decent folk, Dean (of faculty) and Mrs. Franklin Ford who haven't really a clue as to the privilege that is theirs. These are people who simply don't know that a house with a heart is one of

---

175. Elmwood, an eighteenth-century mansion house on the corner of Elmwood Avenue and Mount Auburn Street in Cambridge, is now the official residence of the president of Harvard.

the greatest joys of life. The heart of Elmwood has been carved out and thrown away. Elmwood, a distinguished place for two hundred years; Elmwood, home of Lt Gov. Oliver, of Elbridge Gerry, of James Russell Lowell, of Kingsley Porter has been "suburbanized," brought to a level of mediocrity that is scarcely believable. Today it has all the personality of a hotel room. We have stayed in *motels* that have more charm! Having dined there with the late Mrs. Porter, is only to sigh. Aside from the aridity of the present atmosphere (which could be corrected) there is no excuse whatsoever for the high-handed alteration of the front and back parlor where the dividing fireplace wall had the distinguishing feature of open arches on either side of the chimney breast. Now we have a prosaic door on one side, an equally prosaic wall on the other.

Now all this is bad enough. What really is unconscionable is the fact that Harvard (i.e. [President Nathan] Pusey and Co.) actually entertained the thought of tearing Elmwood down! This was said in plain words by Franklin Ford as we bade him good night and in response to my remark that at least Harvard had not turned the place into an office building full of file cabinets. The excuse offered was the usual Harvard one: Elmwood was weak and crumbling; a fortune is required to hold the fabric together, etc. etc. This was said of Shady Hill.[176] It can be said of any old building (and some new ones!) The shocking thing is that Harvard questions the worth and merit of preserving such tangible legacies from the past. Yet as Elmwood stands today it is a sort of "Harvard ruin." It exists but I cannot say it is alive.

---

176. Shady Hill, formerly the home of Charles Eliot Norton and Paul Sachs, was bought by Harvard and demolished in the 1950s.

7 MARCH 1964

Yesterday to Providence and Newport with Hanns [Swarzenski] and Tom Maytham in the Karolik Lincoln Continental to examine the real property and the contents of the house[177] all of which is responsibility of the MFA to dispose of. The pause in Providence was fruitless as the pictures offered the museum by Malcolm Lovell of New York and housed in a tomb called the Mary Ann Brown building, proved of no interest. The Karolik House (formerly Codman) was a delightful surprise; one of that splendid breed created in the first decade of this century, that age of affluence, elegance, assurance, and taste which also marked the apex of Newport's social brilliance. This Georgian creation, designed by a Codman cousin, Ogden Codman, has some of the air of a C. A. Platt house: formal, well-proportioned, scrupulously detailed, appropriately appointed. The central stair hall of special distinction with its pavement of bright-rimmed marble, its niches with sculpture, its dome and chandelier, pedimented doorways, its sweep of stairs and wrought-iron balustrade. In spite of the bachelor occupancy of twenty years the rooms still have a cheerful, even buoyant look; a fresh coat of paint and the place would be ready for the season. Still I don't really know what you would do with the nearly full-length portrait of Martha Codman's mother in her bridal attire of c. 1850. It is simply too much! Outside the graveled forecourt and the gardens are in perfect order: noble beech trees spreading over clipped paths and rose borders "winterized" to perfection and leading to the tea house which was

---

177. The house in Newport that was designed by Ogden Codman for his cousin Martha was Maxim Karolik's residence until his death in 1964.

copied from the celebrated original designed by McIntire[178] and formerly standing on the Derby estate at Danvers.

But Maxim K[arolik] threw nothing away. The desks in the house were absolutely laden with all the letters of the last twenty years. And all the drawers of every highboy and chest were stuffed with the correspondence and bank statements of years and years. Then there are the nine little stage-coach trunks full of what? In the second floor of the Tea House there are Maxim's fur-trimmed coats, his shirts and cuff-links. Everything![179]

2 MAY 1964

Much too much has happened and time has been too precious to write it down in these pages. The most of the much has been recovery of the great earring, disposal plans of the Karolik estate and the promise of the Forsyth Wickes collection[180] to the MFA. Most dramatic is the first and here the great credit goes to Emily Vermeule who led her B[oston] U[niversity] class in Greek archaeology into the Fens on a "dig" for the earring. Within fifteen minutes one of the class, a Mrs. Wolsky, had "struck gold," i.e. the tin can in which it was buried. Thrills and great rejoicing. Unfortunately I was in New York attending one of the meetings of the Rockefeller Brothers Fund panels on the performing arts and only heard the news upon returning from dinner with Hanns [Swarzenski], Jane Sabersky, and the

---

178. Samuel McIntire, eighteenth-century architect and furniture designer, was one of the finest craftsmen of his period.
179. That year the MFA held a holiday sale of Karolik's effects.
180. The Forsyth Wickes collection of eighteenth-century French paintings, drawings, and decorative arts was given to the MFA in 1964.

Achim Lippes about 12:30 that evening. Telephoned to Diggory Venn[181] in Boston and tried to reach the Vermeules to no avail.

18 MAY 1964

Home from the Tavern dinner for Kingman Brewster, new president of Yale. Kingman, an old Taverner committed himself with refreshing originality and most admirably. He was introduced by Bob Wolff who set a high standard in this art. Determined to tell a Harvard-Yale joke that was irreversible (he maintained, quite rightly that all YH jokes are reversible) he remembered the Barrett Wendell—French Ambassador—one. The Ambassador having just received a Yale degree moved up to Cambridge to take a Harvard one and noted the slight difference between the Yale motto, "Lux et Veritas" and the Harvard's plain "Veritas." Asking Wendell for an explanation, the latter replied simply that at Yale *"La Verite"* was regarded as an *"objet de luxe!"* Brewster spoke at first in a witty verse—the "lost McCord" [Dave McCord] etc. and then basing his remarks upon Lewis Perry's charge to new Taverners which these days is recited as part of Tavern liturgy, spoke warmly of his administration in Yale which would be dedicated to the cultivation of beauty in art and literature. There is no doubt that he intended it as a scolding of Harvard which has fallen in love with bigness. Certainly the present incumbent and his predecessor at Harvard have never spoken of beauty.

---

181. Diggory Venn (1917–1987) held several positions at the MFA under Rathbone—head of education, head of development, and special assistant to the director.

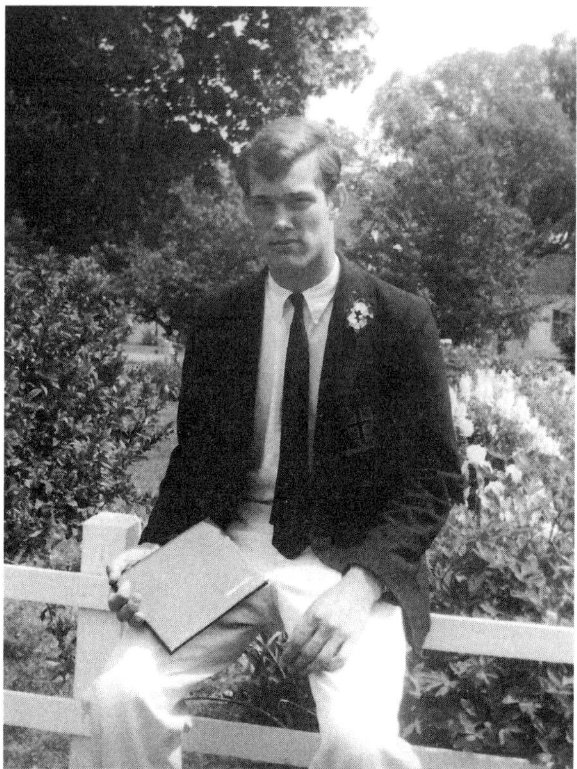

Peter Rathbone poses with his diploma at his graduation from Brooks School in June 1964.

9 JUNE 1964

June will be remembered for Peter's commencement, an event we prayed for. True to his pattern, he squeaked through academically and scored high athletically. He got his diploma, but he also captured the senior athletic prize—a silver bowl. As the prize day awards were announced I kept thinking of the paternal hearts around us—how each and all would hope for the pronouncement of their son's name. And then, because I think one is always better off to expect nothing, my heart really took a jump when I heard "Peter Betts Rathbone." Up stood our handsome, still attractively diffident Peter; a few strides and he was on the platform and modestly accepted what was his most deserving reward—Captain of baseball for two years, Captain of soccer for two years, and junior and senior letters for hockey. Obviously his popularity was second only to his prowess athletically. So we count our blessings and bury our ambitions for Peter as a college student at least for now.

By 3:30 I took off in the "wind-wagon" for Maine, alone, to take an honorary doctorate of Fine Arts from Bates College at Lewiston. Stopped en route at the ancient Poland Spring House to change and refresh before joining President Phillips and the other honorees and trustees of the college for dinner. There I was with Grayson Kirk, President of Columbia University, Yamazaki, architect, Dr. Almus Thorp of Bexley Hall, Kenyon College, William Zorach and wife, and others. A concert in the chapel: Randall Thompson's *Mass of the Holy Spirit*—a sublime composition beautifully sung and a Rachmaninoff suite for two pianos played by honorees Nemenoff and Luboshutz. Then feeling heroic beyond my powers, managed to sit through half of *Henry V*, played by college "thespians."

Fascinated by the colossal wood pile called the Poland Spring House which was the watering place of my great grandparents, i.e. the James L. Connelys. In its heyday it was obviously a "place to meet people" as well as to escape the heat of Philadelphia. Fashion long since turned its back on Poland, but somehow to my amazement, it survives. To be sure they were balancing the books with convention business . . . and

I managed to get the only available room in the old building. My window commanded across a golf course, the lake, and a fine panorama of mountains. But the high ceilings, old plumbing, the verandahs were somehow a picture incomplete without the horses, the carriages. The pomp—however shallow—of another age.

CHÂTEAU DE CASTILLE, ARGILLIERS, GARD
20 JUNE 1964

Darling,

After lunching with the Duchesse de Richelieu[182] on Saturday and going to the ballet at the Opera that night, I closed my Paris chapter for this year and took the express for Avignon Sunday morning. It sounds like a gay time, I know, but actually lunching with the Duchesse was a lot of work and it lasted until 4 PM! She has a way of detaining her guests—more like a jailer than a hostess. How I got there and why is quite a long story but it was in mad pursuit of museum benefaction. My fellow sufferer was [Pierre] Verlet, Decorative Arts curator at the Louvre who certainly was alarmed at my sudden appearance on the scene, so much so that he sent her Grace a large floral arrangement to offset whatever allure I might have had to offer! In spite of the fact she warned me that she might have to leave the table at any moment with *vertige*, we got to the end of the meal without incident. Given the unequivocal statements, she told us she was born with perfect taste!

---

182. The Duchess of Richelieu (1890–1972) was the former Elinor Douglas Wise of Baltimore.

PALAZZO VENIER DEI LEONI, VENEZIA
6 JULY 1964

Dearest Ret,

Here I am again at Peggy's living in the lap of Guggenheim luxury for two and a half days after a wonderful experience fitted in between Paris and Venice. I have just received your letter about the maddening habits of the young. You are right, but I do still remember my own absent-minded ways when I was the age of our three. So they come by it naturally, but they also have to be scolded out of it.

From Paris I took the express to Avignon and one hour later Hanns [Swarzenski] arrived at the Château de Castille. Douglas [Cooper][183] big and noisy and energetic and outrageous but hospitable and fed us well in his Doric dining room. But he was really not prepared to take us to Picasso until I explained that Louise Leiris ([Daniel-Henry] Kahnweiler's sister-in-law) had telephoned days before on our behalf. Then I assumed command, not to be by-passed as the *chef d'opération*. With Picasso it is touch and go, so Hanns and I had our anxieties. But in the end all was well; we made the grade and after a hair-raising, breakneck drive of 270 miles from Avignon to Cannes, we rang at the portal and M. Picasso and Jacqueline came out to greet us with arms open and smiles. But this turned out to be no perfunctory how do you do a look and goodbye but four hours, and after exploring various studios with the maître, the works on the easel and the cavernous studio for sculpture below, P. offered us whiskey and then invited us out to dinner! Hanns and I

---

183. Douglas Cooper (1911–1984) was a controversial British art historian and close friend of Picasso.

glowed with satisfaction as we drove off to a restaurant (Felix) on the shore in Picasso's big car, a driver at the wheel and us two behind. Then a most engaging meal until 11:30! Picasso's eyes are unforgettable and also his delicate tapered fingers. He was like a child in the studio, following all our interests and enthusiasms and bringing out his special treasures for us to enjoy—Degas pastels and the two tiny portraits by Douanier Rousseau. His wife is quite an angel and not to be outdone by Douglas Cooper's effusive kisses, I also asked the privilege of Madame and she responded with unaffected charm. It was too much for Douglas to acknowledge our success. But we had it![184]

Here Peggy has led me through the Biennale and the Dubuffet exhibition at the Palazzo Grassi and last night we dined at Fenicci with the Sutherlands and the Guinesses from Ireland. Now it is late at night and I take the *rapido* in the morning for Florence to rejoin Hanns and Brigitte. All is much too hurried and stimulating. But I am well and strong and like this mad pace for awhile. It is *such* a relaxation from the museum.

2 OCTOBER 1964

Saturday night. The Max Beckmann weekend is coming to a close. Opened show[185] last night with member's reception

---

184. Rathbone and Swarzenski viewed Picasso's *Rape of the Sabine Women* (1963) during their visit. The painting was acquired by the MFA later that year.
185. A Max Beckmann retrospective opened in 1964, co-organized by the Museum of Modern Art, New York, the Museum of Fine Arts, Boston, and the Art Institute of Chicago.

and Max's imposing, problematic art has made a deep impression. A new experience for Boston and the seriousness of the art invoked a serious response. The galleries looked gorgeous filled with the light and color and plastic richness of Beckmann's paint. A French guest said that the colors are happy but the content sad. Sad is not the word, but serious, even ponderous. Lots of guests from out of town: Quappi [Beckmann] of course, looking and feeling radiant won all hearts. Also in the receiving line were H[arold] Joachim of Chicago, Peter Selz and wife of the Museum of Modern Art and Monroe Wheeler of the same; Ralph and Charlotte Lowell and ourselves. Buster May[186] was present, also [Stephen] Lackner from Santa Barbara and Alfred Hentzen from Hamburg, the [Andrew] Ritchies and the [George] Rickeys, Jane Sabersky and the [Catherine] Vivianos, and Stanley Seeger of New York. Everyone agreed they had never seen Beckmann so superbly manifested and I was very proud and happy.

Dinner for eighteen here before reception which included Peter for first time, Sue Herter and Kate Avery Clark, the Ritchies, and the Charles Kuhns[187] and Seymour Slives.[188] A well-mixed party. Afterwards a night-cap here until 2 A.M.

Busy day with guests from out of town. Lunch with Quappi and Joachim. Wally Barker[189] for dinner and much talk of

---

186. Morton "Buster" May (1914–1983), of the May department store company headquartered in St. Louis, assembled an exceptionally large collection of Max Beckmann's work, which he subsequently donated to the St. Louis Art Museum.

187. Charles Kuhn (1902–1985) was curator of Harvard's Busch-Reisinger Museum of Germanic Art from 1930 to 1968.

188. Seymour Slive (1920–2014) was an art history professor at Harvard and an expert in seventeenth-century Dutch painting.

189. Wally Barker (1921–2004), a St. Louis artist, was a friend and student of Max Beckmann at Washington University.

extra-sensory perception induced by drugs, Max's premonitory instincts and fantastic symbolism.

6 OCTOBER 1964

Busy all day with the greatest living portrait photographer, Yousuf Karsh of Ottawa. This fabled artist whose work I have admired for years came Sunday with Ivan Dimitri of New York to "case" the museum and meet me there preparatory to doing my portrait today. He is an intense short man with big bulbous eyes and nose, a bald head, and a gray fringe of longish hair around it. Quick and elastic in his movements, in spite of some sixty years I guess, he cuts a wide swath with his vision and responds eagerly and quickly to all he sees and feels. A tour of the whole main floor of the museum is a lot for one and a half hours but Karsh was equal to it.

Today he posed me in five galleries—amongst the impressionists, in front of the Greco and Fra Felix, the R. van der Weyden, the Boston "throne," and a niche in the hemicycle. Mr. K. has a lot of charm at his fingertips, displayed extraordinary patience and a power of concentration that impressed me very much. He has a trick of bringing you to keen attention at the crucial moment of the shutter by whispering, "Beautiful, do not move at all!" Then he says "Dear Sir, look here, head down, look there, etc." His English is almost perfect, but with a middle eastern accent. He is an Armenian. Of course he has a kind of sixth sense. His antennae are tuned to personality and I felt all day that I was undergoing an analytical study. He must have used up a hundred plates on me, and interspersed them with Polaroid shots for the first time—to take a "reading" on what he was doing. While he worked, the tireless [Ivan] Dimi-

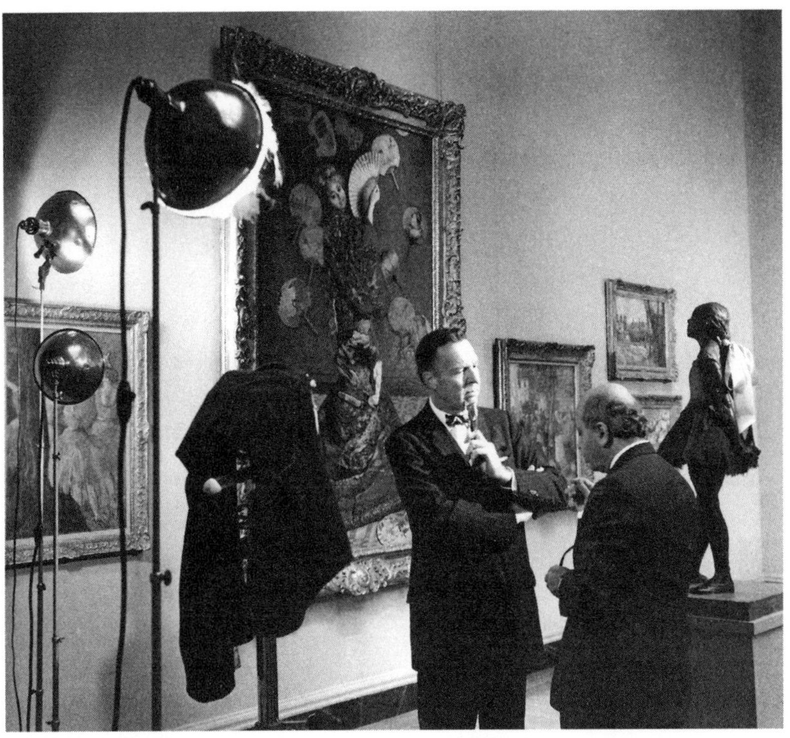

Rathbone takes direction in a portrait session with Yousuf Karsh in the Impressionist gallery at the MFA in October 1964.

tri made endless candid shots of the operation. Mr. K. has elegant taste, perfectly pressed suit, conspicuous cuff buttons and initials on the cuff! "Now you are speaking to a friend": "Now your thoughts are far away, not on the present," he was fond of saying. At 7 P.M. at last we made the final exposure and I invited both Dimitri and Karsh home for cocktails with Hanns and Brigitte [Swarzenski]. K. was enraptured by Hanns' splendid face and head, and Brigitte's also. Obviously they wanted to stay with them, so they left together.

9 OCTOBER 1964

Last Saturday Olivier Bès de Berc of Paris came to the museum where I met him. He's a young engineer involved with aluminum and had come from Pittsburgh. Only member of his family now interested in art. Takes after his great grandfather who formed the collection from which we bought *Martyrdom of St. Hippolytus.* He told me that ten years ago Georges Wildenstein had approached his father and seen the triptych and then offered to buy it for $10,000 and to have a copy of it made for Mr. B. de B. "Please get out" was the response. Mr. O. allowed that he did not think he was a very honest man.

Yesterday passed by the former residence[190] of the late Adelaide Marquand. It is absolutely flattened by the house-wreckers. This wooden colossus with its two-story classic order and its porte-cochere has suddenly disappeared. Mrs. M. was found in a bathtub of water some months ago. Little did I think that I had paid my last visit to that mansion when with Gardner Cox we put her to bed (after dinner here), pulled out her hairpins and took off her earrings. Sic transit gloria mundi.

15 OCTOBER 1964

Dinner at the [Frederick] Deknatels'[191] in Brattle st. A party for Kenneth and Eleanor Murdock, lately of I Tatti, Florence;

---

190. The Marquand house stood at the corner of Reservoir and Fayerweather streets in Cambridge.
191. Frederick B. Deknatel (1905–1973) was a professor in Harvard's Department of Fine Arts from 1940 to 1972, a medievalist with a keen interest in modern art.

in fact, the first director. An aspirant for the Harvard presidency, Kenneth was given I Tatti as delayed consolation, it is said, for his disappointment. Also the Kaplans and Betty Miller (Perry Miller's widow) were on hand for a very agreeable evening. Khrushchev has resigned[192] and the rest of the world has jitters and the stock market dips way down. I myself can only believe that a further rupture in East-West relations will eventually come about.

John Goelet[193] here momentarily; a visit with him in my office for forty minutes and he whisked off. He is surely the busiest unemployed man in the world. Brigitte Swarzenski in New England Baptist Hospital for gallbladder operation. All's well.

Last weekend at the Cape to close our cottage #6. Drove down on a bright Saturday. But the wind came up in the evening and though we had an ocean dip in the late afternoon sun, the cold had set in and we slept under four blankets and a comforter each. We kept the hearth fire at full blast until bedtime. Worked hard on my Beckmann lecture. Next A.M. Betty [Chace] insisted we come up to the big house to keep warm, dine, and sleep and we were happy to accept. Winchesters also with us. But the sea was glassy calm in the afternoon and the sun was bright, so I swam again because the water was irresistible. Wonderful steak dinner with the Chaces and Winchesters, but

---

192. Following a decline in Khrushchev's popularity the Politburo in fact voted to remove him from office on October 14, 1964. He was replaced by Leonid Brezhnev as the new leader of the Communist Party.

193. John Goelet (1931–2023), an innovative businessman and patron of the arts, was a "field representative" to the Asiatic Department and later a trustee of the MFA during Rathbone's tenure. With his home base near Paris, he often joined Rathbone and Hanns Swarzenski during their European sojourns.

just as we were to sit down, Georgie, the black poodle, tangled with a skunk and Betty was obliged to bathe him in quarts of tomato juice, then soap and water before we got on with dinner. [Barry] Goldwater,[194] the Chace family favorite—hard to believe—was never mentioned, so I think Malcolm and Betty have given up hope on this unfortunate aspirant to the most powerful seat in the world.

Next day loaded up the Peugeot—to the ceiling—with bags and blankets and provisions and every kind of family odds and ends and lush remainders from Betty's garden—parsley and lettuce and roses. And a bucket of blue mussels. Sad farewell to the Cape and a long and happy chapter in our family life. Next year Peter will be in Army and Ret and I expect to be in Europe. And cottage #6, so familiar for years, may be sold to other owners by this time next year. The Cape changes—how swiftly! I see a complete surrender of the holdings of the old Yankee higher order and a ruination of the "Old Cape" we have loved.

Yesterday a cocktail party at the John Coolidges for Miss [Emily] Rauh[195] who is about to leave for St. Louis as curator of the City Art Museum.

---

194. Barry Goldwater (1909–1998) ran for president in 1964 and lost in a landslide to Lyndon Johnson.
195. Emily Rauh was assistant curator of drawings at the Fogg Art Museum at Harvard from 1957 to 1964 when she left to become curator at the St. Louis Art Museum. She married Joseph Pulitzer Jr. in 1973. His first wife, Louise Vauclain, died in 1968.

29 OCTOBER 1964

This is the eve of Peter's departure for the army[196] and he confesses to having "butterflies" in the stomach. He is off to Fort Dix in the morning from the recruiting headquarters in Central Square.

Jack Newberry[197] died in Paris a week ago on October 23rd. Found dead in his bed at the Hotel Lancaster in the morning. Thus ends a friendship of over thirty years. Thus Eliza's godfather passes from the scene when she is only sixteen and thus I am separated from the friend who introduced me to my first museum job in 1934. This dear fellow, so spoiled and self-indulgent was the victim of drink, a weakness accentuated by his mother's death five or six years ago from which he never recovered. He apparently thought he might die abroad, for he had left explicit instructions for closing out his earthly term and this his brother Cammann, having flown to Paris, is taking care of.

14 NOVEMBER 1964

Last evening Quappi Beckmann and her sister Hedda Schoonderbeek of Ohlstadt, Bavaria, came to dinner and

---

196. Peter volunteered for a three-year European theater stint in the army after graduating from Brooks School, having been advised to postpone college and avoid being drafted for the war in Vietnam.

197. John "Jack" Newberry (1910–1964) was a classmate of Rathbone's at Harvard and fellow graduate of Paul Sachs' museum course. He helped to secure Rathbone's first job at the Detroit Institute of Arts, where he was curator of graphic arts.

afterwards we were joined by two younger eager enthusiasts of Max's art: Dr. Paul Lee and Mr. Chapman. These young men, pupils of Tillich and Erik Erikson are deeply involved with the metaphysics of MB's painting and eagerly want to probe it to its depths from their point of view. In spite of their great respect for Max's artistic statements, they are prone to see symbolism in every stroke of his brush.

To the museum at 10 on this Saturday morning to meet a pair of Texans, Messrs. Bird and Scott to consult with me about the new Kimbell Art Foundation at Fort Worth. The Kimbell will yield conservatively $2,000,000 per annum for operating and acquisitions. In other words a new threat in the ever-increasing competition for great works of art.

18 NOVEMBER 1964

Yesterday Diggory Venn and I went to Boston College to meet Secretary of the Interior Stewart Udall, to beard him before his lecture before the RC seminar, to place in his hands a three-page statement about the inner-belt outrage,[198] to speak to him about the threat to the MFA, Gardner Museum, Simmons College, Emmanuel College, Wentworth Institute and

---

198. The "Inner Belt" was proposed as an eight-lane highway that would have torn through parts of Cambridge and Boston, displacing thousands of residents and destroying urban parklands. The controversial proposal lingered throughout the 1960s until it was finally defeated through the efforts of neighborhood groups and city leaders pleading with politicians. Rathbone was involved in the effort as the director of the MFA, which would have suffered with the "Inner Belt" in its own backyard. Ultimately the money allocated for the "Inner Belt" was redirected toward public transportation in the extension of the Red Line to Alewife and the relocation of the Orange Line.

our own school. He was receptive to our plea, asked pertinent questions. Most importantly, he said he was to be given veto powers by the Congress in January that could have vital bearing on Inner Belt and recreation land-taking and dissolution of "integrated land use." Francis Sargent,[199] a youngish, toothsome operator and Commissioner of the D[epartment] of I[nterior] tried to mar our message —quite rudely—by stating that the road had to be built no matter what. Later, everything Mr. [Secretary] had to say was a leading statement against the proposed route of the Inner Belt. Time was not wasted: perhaps it's the beginning of a real defense.

Today a gorgeous crystalline day—to Topsfield with Hanns [Swarzenski] to view the [Edward Jackson] Holmes property and to select objects for the museum. How beautiful the countryside! Not so much could be said for the younger legatee, Mrs. Margaretta Davis of Baltimore. After several hours of looking and considering and deciding on this, that, or the other with Hanns, Mrs. D. decided that "art" in Mrs. Holmes' will did not include furniture. And telephoned the attorney, Schipper, for clarification. Mrs. Davis, a spoiled and avaricious young woman, a person whose face spells anxiety and discontent seems determined to try to frustrate the clear instructions of Mrs. Holmes' will.

---

199. Francis Sargent (1915–1998) was to become governor of Massachusetts from 1969 to 1975, by which time he had changed his tune and in fact stood out for his environmental policies. He was instrumental in redirecting "Inner Belt" funds to public transportation.

9 DECEMBER 1964

Opening of the Hirshhorn[200] Collection at Museum this afternoon following monthly meeting of trustees. And following that, dinner at home for eighteen guests to honor the uranium king and collector, the self-made East-side boy who buys art by the bagful and loves it with an all-embracing enthusiasm. On hand was his wife #4,[201] a modest, lovely woman who can obviously take Joe, at least for now. We also had to entertain his "disturbed" adopted daughter (second marriage) who is now resident at McLain Hospital and her swain. All of this was not exactly calculated to put Rett the hostess at ease, but she carried it off beautifully. And the party was a great success with [John] McAndrews, young [Charles] Cunninghams, [Hanns and Brigitte] Swarzenskis, [David] Bakalars, [Jeptha] Wades, Morgans, John Coolidges. This was our first cocktail preview subscription at the museum. About five hundred members turned up. And many agreed that *this* was the dinner.

---

200. Joseph Hirshhorn (1899–1981) was a voracious collector of contemporary art. Rathbone might have hoped that hosting an exhibition of his collection would lead to important donations to the MFA, but Hirshhorn ultimately gave his entire collection to the Smithsonian Institution in 1966 and the creation of his own eponymous museum on the Mall of Washington, DC, which opened in 1974.
201. Olga Zatorsky

15 JANUARY 1965

Tues. Forsyth Wickes[202] died unexpectedly and I felt obliged to go to the funeral in New York two days before Christmas. Took midnight sleeper and flew back next day after service in St. James' where the other "art mourners" included Charlie Cunningham,[203] Fred Adams of the Morgan Library, Ted Rousseau and last but also first, Agnes Mongan. Now I live in anxiety about the settlement of his will, as he explained to me that in case of his death his collection's disposition would be in the hands of a committee of his family. After trimming the Christmas tree with Bee, spent the eve of the great day writing a letter of condolence to Mrs. Wickes and got to bed by 3 A.M. This was perhaps our last Xmas with all three children. Peter home from Basic Training in the army in Fort Dix with head shaven, but nevertheless very handsome in his uniform. Eliza growing more beautiful again and wonderfully poised for sixteen. Our children show us great and genuine affection which is the deepest satisfaction parents can have. Peter's maturity is catching up with Eliza's which has been precocious. That they like us and our company and that of our friends means everything. Deeply conservative, even worshipful of family festive customs, everything for Christmas was comme il faut: the stockings ever, the big tree with everything, but everything, on it, presents in the morning after breakfast after stockings on the parental bed. Then dressing and our beloved friends for

---

202. Forsyth Wickes was a collector of French art of the eighteenth century; Rathbone was actively courting him for the MFA.

203. Charles Cunningham (1910–1979), Rathbone's Harvard classmate, was assistant curator of paintings at the MFA from 1934 to 1946 and then director of the Wadsworth Atheneum in Hartford, Connecticut, from 1946 to 1966.

the feast: Hanns and Brigitte and Jan and Yvonne Cox. Rettles still in last stages of fearful cold and Brigitte still a bit of a convalescent after her operation, our guests left us at about 7 P.M. after a little conservative dancing—not the fandangos, minuets, and polkas of other years—not yet again! One of the sensations of the day was Jan's beautiful charcoal and pastel portrait of Belinda. This lovely work pleases all, including Bee. It *is* a likeness of face and mood and very distinguished as a work of art. As always, the sun came out and brightened the day.

30 SEPTEMBER 1965

Months of neglect stare me in the face. The ever-increasing pressure of life puts writing a journal almost beyond endurance. Time and again since February the impulse has been smothered by fatigue. Tonight we opened the [Nicolas] de Staël exhibition—first large-scale, comprehensive show to be seen in America. And it bears out all my deep faith in the man. His genuine mastery of vision and means are everywhere apparent. For sheer vitality one can compare him only with Van Gogh.

Dinner party here for nineteen before going on to the Museum. The Messers from the Guggenheim, Agooses, and young Gimpel, Cunningham jrs., Eloise Spaeth, Lord and Lady Gowrie, Mrs. Hammacher from Rotterdam, Wades, Maythams, and the new French consul general Massenet and wife. Ret did a very good dinner of Boeuf Bourguignon and we had an excellent Margaux. Tom Messer gave gallery talk in P.M. Crowd was so great he had to stand on a chair to be seen and make himself heard. But he fell off the chair, sprained an ankle, had to be bandaged and treated gently. But he manfully stood up in receiving line with faithful Ralph and Charlotte Lowell, the Allan MacNabs of Chicago, Remi Messer and ourselves.

The Forsyth Wickes collection is ours! Two days ago word came from the family that here in the MFA it would repose. This is the end of a long and anxious period. Our chief rivals seem to have been Hartford and the Art Institute of Chicago. But to Boston it will come, just as Wickes wanted it to come, tho' he had never seen the Museum. Instead of building the Wickes collection into our five year plan, culminating in 1970 for our centennial, we must proceed at once. Mrs. Wickes is getting on and would like to see the collection transferred from Newport and installed.[204]

3 OCTOBER 1965

Home from a weekend in the Berkshires with Pinky Carroll[205] and the George Rickeys and a great family picnic-reunion at Shaker Village en route. There we gathered at noon from three cities: New York, Providence, and Cambridge—Don and Zorka, Roly and Eliot Nolen, Malcolm and Betty and ourselves with Bee. Rollicking lunch in the open air on the lee-side of the big shop-laundry building, for the autumn wind was coolish though the sun was bright. Then a tour of the village with Amy Bess Miller, the guiding light of the restoration enterprise. Something very touching about the deeply cultivated simplicity of these people, and their sense of design a

204. The Forsyth Wickes galleries at the MFA opened in 1968, with the collections installed to approximate the Wickes' arrangements at Starboard House in Newport, Rhode Island. In later years the collection was disbursed to various departments within the museum.
205. Georgia "Pinky" Carroll was the widow of John Carroll, both of them artists and friends dating back to Rathbone's Detroit years. Pinky was friend and neighbor to George and Edie Rickey in East Chatham, New York.

matter of great taste. Realized for first time that the Shakers sang their own archaic a capella hymns as they danced away their sins at Sunday worship, that children—usually orphans—lived amongst them and that they were traveling salesmen of their own products. Great round barn is most urgent problem—and most expensive. Its masonry walls are now shoved up against imminent collapse. About $350,000 is needed for restoration.

27 OCTOBER 1965

Today we had our first "cultivation meeting" for the Centennial Development Fund drive. A luncheon party arranged by Mrs. Paul Bernat[206] for a group of prospects. A bit of a strain for all concerned. But anxiety melted with the success of the proceedings. Mrs. B. spoke beautifully and Ralph Lowell was at his best. Then a slide presentation with a tape record followed by my speech which went over very well. We are encouraged. For the first time outside the Museum family I pronounced our need—$20,000,000.[207]

9 NOVEMBER 1965

The Museum's benefit premier performance of the movie, *The Agony and the Ecstasy*[208] was rubbed out tonight by the elec-

---

206. Paul and Helen Bernat were collectors of Asian art and important patrons of the MFA. Helen Bernat, along with Frannie Hallowell, was one of the first women to join the MFA's board of trustees.
207. Equivalent to approximately $191,000,000 in 2023
208. The 1965 movie version of Irving Stone's epic biography of

trical power failure that extended throughout the Northeast.[209] It hit Boston and the Museum at 5:30 as my curtain speech was being typed. Made my way home from a blacked-out Boston by the light of the moon and my car headlights to find Arthur Brooks[210] already chez nous for dinner, but sitting round the drawing room hearth with Ret by firelight and candlelight uncertain of the entire evening. Incapacitated electric stove meant a cold supper of ham and salad preceded by soup, heated in the fireplace. With no light by 9:30, program canceled, and we resigned ourselves to a most enjoyable quiet evening at home. Some thirty pre-performance dinner parties were similarly paralyzed. Frequent telephone communications with theatre. Finally gave over the evening at 9:30. At ten electric illumination resumed after four and a half hours of darkness

Jan Fontein[211] left for Amsterdam tonight. Another interview today. Believe he will accept our invitation to join staff. But still the decision waits upon his consultation with wife. Everybody seems to like him as much as I did from the start. And he has been wined and dined—and even waltzed—all the ten days of his stay.

Michelangelo

209. The great Northeast blackout affected about thirty million people.

210. Arthur Brooks, an architect, and his wife Jean were friends and neighbors of the Rathbones in Cambridge.

211. Rathbone was interviewing Jan Fontein (1927–2017) of the Rijksmuseum, Amsterdam, for the position of curator of Asian art at the MFA. Fontein accepted the job in 1966 and went on to become director of the MFA from 1975 to 1987.

7 DECEMBER 1965

My debt, given the outcome, to Paul Sachs may have been greater than that of his many students.[212] I hope—and I think I did—I hope I discharged it. Though, I must say, having already written very personally about him in the MFA bulletin, I feel I had done so. Nevertheless my words were from the heart.

Have simply not had the time, nor strength when the day was over, to add a line to this book for two or three weeks. Tho' every day was more interesting than that of most people in a month. One week ago Jim Rorimer of the Met came to see me unexpectedly: to ask if Dus Cavallo could help him catalogue the Metropolitan collection of medieval tapestries. This is one of the world's great collections. Humble pie for the Met to ask Boston to catalogue same. Of course. Ask Cavallo to do anything you want. That is for him to decide. Good for him, good for the MFA if he can spare the time. But it was obvious that J. R. was deeply perturbed. His curator of the Cloisters, Tom Hoving,[213] was leaving him, leaving the profession; going into "politics." Hoving has long confided to Hanns Swarzenski that he couldn't stand Rorimer. So it's easy to imagine that this was a way out. Rorimer asked, "would Randall[214] come back to the Cloisters?" I thought "No." Poor tortured Rorimer, he defeats himself with his self-importance, with his secrecy, with

212. Rathbone delivered a speech at a tribute to Paul Sachs, who had died earlier that year, during the *Paul J. Sachs Memorial Exhibition* at the Fogg Art Museum.
213. Thomas Hoving (1931–2009) became New York parks commissioner in 1966 before returning to the Metropolitan Museum as director from 1967 to 1977 at the death of James Rorimer.
214. Randall was a curator at the Cloisters before becoming assistant curator of decorative arts at the MFA from 1959 to 1964.

his arrogance born of insecurity. I had not the heart to tell him that Jan Fontein had accepted our invitation to become curator of Asiatic art. Fontein told me he had turned down the Metropolitan last year.

Constantly in the throes of fund-raising organization. Another meeting today. First of the Centennial Development Council: two and a half hours. The Council is fixed, not by Ralph Lowell's fiat, but by my importunity. But still we have no chairman, though I have personally solicited Richard Chapman and John Wilson. We sigh for a leader.

With these problems on my mind, commenced the day with a meeting with Bradford Washburn[215] at his house in Sparks St. this morning at 8:30.

9 DECEMBER 1965

Last evening dined at Leverett Saltonstall's[216] house in Dover and got lost trying to find it. He and Alison were entertaining at a small dinner for Mme Chiang Kai-shek.[217] I met this well-bred and proper seductress for the first time and immediately upon entering the living room, already peopled with the Bill Claflins, Charles Cabots, Catherine Coolidge, Sinclair Weeks, and the courtier-like nephew of N.Y. and Miami, was seated

---

215. Bradford Washburn (1910–2007), a mountaineer and photographer, was founder and director of Boston's science museum from 1951 to 1980.

216. Leverett Saltonstall (1892–1979) was US Senator from Massachusetts from 1945 to 1967.

217. Soong Mei-ling (1898–2003) was the second wife of Chiang Kai-shek and notably helped him to advocate for traditional Chinese values and to establish his government in Taiwan following the civil war between Nationalists and Communists in mainland China.

next to her by the Senator. Sleek and graceful, smooth as satin in manner, voice, movement. She has a most agreeable, polished accent that falls on the ear like liquid pearls. She remembers your name and pronounces it right. She is warm, almost subversive but does not love her dignity, never gives herself away. Obviously does not know much about Chinese art and was not planning a visit to the MFA this trip tho' had not been there for thirty years. She is miraculously preserved. Wellesley class of 1917 means she must be about seventy, but she looks about fifty-five! Can't agree with her politics. She advocates dropping nuclear bombs on Vietcong targets! Later learned through connection at the *Globe* this was an error. But together we spoke of art and the rehabilitation of crippled children, her principal interest and charity.

16 DECEMBER 1965

The "big event" was a surprise party for me at the museum to celebrate my tenth anniversary. I, the unsuspecting victim, was led to the "slaughter" by Rettles who turned out to be the most subtle actress of them all in this colossal conspiracy. With utter quiet she drove me to the museum, black tie, with the subterfuge of meeting the John McDonnells there to change cars and proceed to a dinner party at # 9 Knox St. But upon alighting at the rendezvous in front of the Huntington Ave entrance, the portal was thrown open and there, standing on the stairs to greet me, were two hundred friends—trustees, staff, Ladies Committee past and present, in evening dress and a red carpet spread from top to bottom and everyone crying "syncharitiria" (congratulations). Incredulous, dumbfounded, my first thought as I mounted the stairs with Ret was that I would have to give a

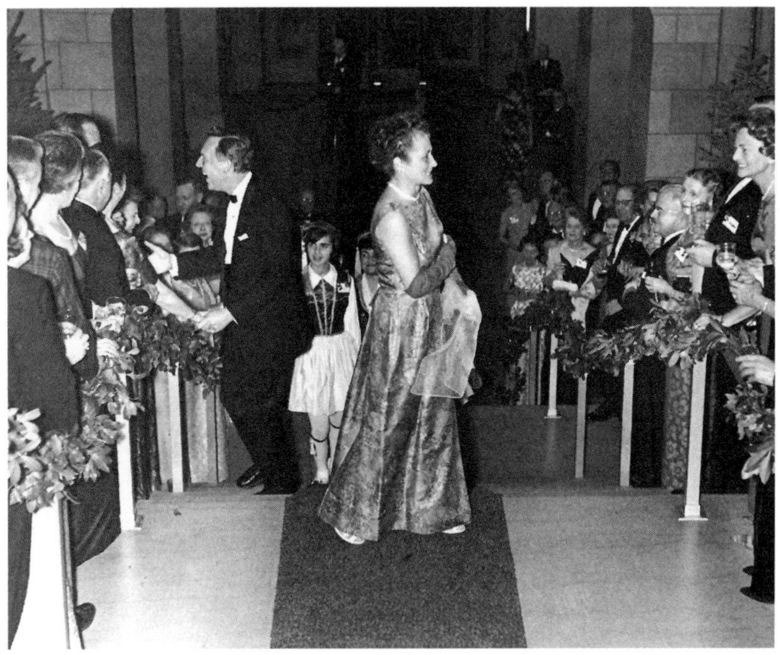

Rathbone and Rettles Rathbone greet guests at a surprise party honoring Rathbone's tenth anniversary as director of the MFA in December 1965.

speech! And how could I do justice to the occasion? At the top of the stairs I was crowned with laurels by Ralph Lowell and the next moment a waiter flashed into sight with two glasses of iced ouzo, then congratulations on all sides, general cocktail hubbub in the Rotunda followed by a dinner dance in the Tapestry Hall. A Greek menu[218] and retsina, speeches, a

218. It was well known that Rathbone had developed a passion for Greece during his first visit in 1961 (see letter to Rettles from June 1961) and from then on made a habit of returning to Greece every summer, ever striving to improve on his modern Greek and Greek dancing—and enjoying the food and wine.

divertissement by six members of the ladies committee with [George] Peabo Gardner[219] as MC—and a perfect one. I managed to phrase a few thoughts in Greek by way of introduction to the amusement of the company, esp. the Greek band. Then Greek dances after dinner, a foxtrot and waltzes too. The evening had a genius hard to define. But everyone agreed it was there. Woven through it all was the spirit, personality, the imagination of Frannie Hallowell.[220] Especially pleased to see Alvan and Lee Fuller[221] who had come days early from Palm Beach to be on hand. In a long but serious moment of confidence, "Persh" allowed that they would give the great late Rembrandt to the Museum. When I admitted that I had intended to ask for the painting as a centennial gift he asked when the centennial came. "1970" said I, with confidence. "We won't wait that long" he answered. No doubt the spirit of the moment inspired the resolution. One cannot underestimate the importance of such events.

5 MAY 1966

The great Matisse opening. We had dinner party for twenty-two, packed with old friends—Joe Kellehers from Princeton, Robert Osborns from Salisbury, Conn., the Ted Hilles'[222] from New Haven, Mrs. Anne Barrett. Mrs. Paul

---

219. George Peabody Gardner (1917–2012), a collateral descendent of Isabella Stewart Gardner, was a loyal patron of the MFA.

220. Francis Weeks Hallowell was the first woman trustee of the MFA; she founded the Ladies Committee with Rathbone in 1955.

221. Alvan Fuller Jr. of Palm Beach was son of automobile dealer and one-time governor of Massachusetts Alvan T. Fuller.

222. Frederick Hilles (1900–1975) was a professor of English literature at Yale; his wife Susan Morse Hilles (1905–2002) was a collector of contemporary art. That she was once a student at the School of the

Matisse came but husband in hospital with kidney stone. The [Edouard] Morot-Sirs were guests of honor as cultural attaché of the French Embassy. Also Joe and Lulu Pulitzer and the Swarzenskis, Jane Sabersky and Roland Belay and the Lewis Cabots, Dan Coolidge and Randall Thompson. About thirteen hundred people turned up at the Museum and we did a Spartan duty of shaking hands with guests for nearly an hour! The show is a huge success, probably my greatest since coming to Boston. Rettles very stunning in her new blue and white print evening dress—the one I gave her for Eliza's coming out.

30 JANUARY 1967

Most of the day doing TV program on Age of Rembrandt[223] for WNAC—a half hour in color. Nothing can be more time-consuming than TV—both to create and to watch. I had sat up until 2 A.M. two nights earlier, dictating into my machine my comments on certain paintings. Commencing at about 10 A.M. I had already spent four hours preparing this half hour program. Even though all my "tapings" were right on the first "go," still I spent another three hours on this program.

"Rembrandt" Exhibition coasts along on huge attendance— nearly fifty thousand already and three thousand catalogues sold.

Museum of Fine Arts made for a bond with Boston that Rathbone did his utmost to cultivate. He hosted an exhibition of works from her collection in 1966. In the end she disbursed her collection to several museums, including the MFA.
223. "The Age of Rembrandt" was a blockbuster exhibition shared by the Museum of Fine Arts, Boston, The Toledo Museum of Art, and the California Palace of the Legion of Honor, San Francisco, in 1966-1967.

31 JULY 1967

A big bash at the Museum—dinner for the Mayors of the US—their wives with our own admirable John Collins as host. Sadly many of the principal executives of the country were absent, last minute cancellations owing to racial strife, riots, across the U.S.[224] I sat next to Mayor of New Orleans, a most forthcoming chap with a very creole name. We exchanged pleasantries regarding my old friend and colleague James Byrnes, director of the Delgado Museum there. Then I spoke of conspiracy—the Kennedy assassination plot; should we have credence; was it possible? What of Shaw[225] and the others? Wham! Mayor Schiro came back with more than plus. He believes totally in the theory of plot vs. the solo performance of Oswald. Has known Shaw for years; is familiar with his peculiar background, his homosexuality and the rest. But recognizes that he has nothing to gain from his revelations. In the District attorney whose name is Garrison he has absolute confidence as a man of integrity, not looking for spot light or headlines. But like him, the mayor believes information of a vital kind has been withheld from the American public by pressure from the Kennedy family. According to his theory the family wishes all to believe that the President was the victim of a single crackpot, not of the organized plan of a dissident group. For the family, the case is a closed book making the president an unqualified hero, sacrificed by a single obscure crackpot whose motives

224. 1967 was known as "the long, hot summer" for its more than 150 race riots in cities across the USA.
225. Clay Shaw (1913–1974), a New Orleans businessman, was charged and brought to trial in 1967 for conspiring to assassinate John F. Kennedy. He was found not guilty.

were muddled. The N[ew] O[rleans] view is that murder will out and that it will be found that Oswald was the tool of irate Cuban refugees whose friends and kin were involved in the desperate fiasco of the Bay of Pigs assault. Assured of victory by secret American support they were left unprotected and lost their lives or were taken prisoner. Holding the president personally responsible, these men sought revenge and implicated Oswald who sought the president's life for reasons of his own. Ruby was involved after the fact and his wife received the benefit. This theory in general fits the attitude of most Europeans about the assassination. Our friends abroad could never accept the idea that Oswald was a solo murderer. And if it were true, it must be admitted that his shot alone was next to miraculous. Anyway, as the mayor knows, the case is not closed; and his old D.A. only wants to prove that vital information has been kept from us.

8 AUGUST 1967

A weekend at Cape Cod. First stop, Mrs. Fritz Talbot in Wiano. This charming and warm hearted old dame was genius behind the Cape Cod Art Association Ball—a headdress affair to raise money. I was one of three judges with Mrs. Donald David and an artist-musician type called Celantino. My evening at the Club Wiano was effectively ruined by the obligation involved: a review of all the assembled heads and what was on them! Dreadful assignment. Our post-observation deliberations were interrupted when Mrs. Rose Kennedy sailed up and greeted me. While she wore nothing on her head, she could have taken a prize for the most expensive evening gown of the evening—and a pretty one, made of pink satin. She was very cordial. We dined at the Felix Duponts' at Oyster Harbors. Climax of the meal was superlative boiled salmon which Mrs. D. had recently taken in the waters of a Norway fjord. I rather liked the ultra-American atmosphere and taste of this house after many weeks in Europe.

24 AUGUST 1967

Phase #2 of our building program now under way in the Museum. Steam shovels in the East Court make life hell for those around it. The entire area will become storage for Classical and Egypt Departments—a new and vital underground. But it's like rebuilding the roofs—which has fallen to my lot— nothing that shows for all the money spent!

Yesterday during our garden meal, about 7:30 a young man with long sideburns appeared with a petition to enjoin the common council of Cambridge to protest the Vietnam War. I can't imagine it will have effect; but Rett and I enthusiastically signed it for both of us are anti the present provocation of the war which seems to us a worthless expenditure of lives and money. Young man—Harvard graduate student—had reached same conclusion and wished to make sacrifice of time and effort, saying it was nothing compared with that of the young men overseas.

Lawlessness is on the increase, and to an extent I have never known in our country. After twelve years of security, our house was broken into just before my return from Europe. Three young boys were suspected by the police. They broke in the drawing room door by smashing a pane of glass and turning the knob. Fortunately they were bent not on destruction, but on finding cash and booze. They made off with gin and beer and all the cash in the coin savings bank and my Dunhill table lighter—a silver object inscribed to me with my name from the museum ten years ago. Now I contemplate a burglar alarm. Entry record on the one day or night that Alan Cohen, our student dish washer and handy man, was absent this summer.

16 JUNE 1968
SEMIRAMIS HOTEL, CAIRO

Darling,

Cairo at last and with constant thoughts of you. My windows overlook the Nile and the island where you lived.[226] The Sporting Club has been pointed out ten times already.

Cairo is far bigger than I expected, busier and noisier too. But also better looking with its mud colored architecture, graceful bridges and verdant river fronts. It teems with cars and people. The latter swarm all over everything, especially at night along the Nile promenade: on the revetment, on the sidewalk, around the bread and bean vendors and all over the ground. Of course it's hot. The sun is fierce and goes down white behind the palm trees of your Gezirah. I have moved into an air-conditioned room which makes sleeping a bit easier.

While the Semiramis has a certain tone, it is obviously not the spruce and fashionable place it once was—when Mimi and Lord Allenby were waltzing around. But it's filled with

---

226. Rettles Rathbone was born in Cairo in 1909 and spent the first ten years of her life there. Her father, Claude de Cosson, was head of public works. They lived on Gezirah, a quiet residential island in the middle of Cairo.

servants, tall Nubians in flowing galabeas, and Arabs who handle the breakfast trays. The servants, the heat, and the pyramids are the only things that haven't changed since your day here, I suppose.

I arrived in the cool of midnight—surprisingly comfortable. The airport of the city is a strange second class place that inspires no confidence in the new arrival. It took a relay of three bearers and a door opener to get me into my cab. Driver of the latter knew one word of English which was "bowen." This turned out to be "pound"—one pound for the taxi ride! I looked up Ed Terrace[227] who came rushing over to the Semiramis bar where we drank beer till 2 am and caught up on all the diplomatique news, the scotching of the Metropolitan threat and we lined up maneuvers for the morrow. Pat and Edmundo [LaSalle] are fine and seem to thrive on Egypt.

In the morning we called on a sub-cultural propaganda minister with clipped Oxford accent in Gezirah, up river a way, past the Sport Club (maybe near your house) and planned our attack on the Director of Antiquities. Then to the Egyptian Museum to see Dr. [Henry] Riad [Ghabur], Director. He was all smiles in his dusty old office, but he shies away from making decisions about possible precious loans.[228] Then he led us forth into the colossal mess which is his museum. The normal jam packed confusion is compounded by the "war time" measure of sand bags and taped glass on

---

227. Edward Terrace (1936–1973) had recently been appointed associate curator of Egyptian art at the MFA.

228. At the time Rathbone was in the midst of preparing an exhibition of Egyptian treasures from the Cairo Museum for the MFA jointly with the Metropolitan Museum for their centennials in 1970. Cairo cancelled the show at the last minute due to a spate of airplane hijackings in the Middle East.

all the cases, some of the major pieces are half concealed with heaped up bags, some of them spilling their sand around the monuments so that they look the way they did when excavated! The museum itself is terrible beyond my wildest dreams. Dirty, cheerless, dead. One half of the collection should be in storage. But first of all they should pull the building down and start over again.

We lunched at Shepherd's Roof (next to Semiramis) and slept the balance of the afternoon.

This morning (Sunday) we went out to Giza to the pyramids, a sight that sways the mind and the imagination as nothing else but the Parthenon. I was spellbound by the majesty, the magnitude, and the beauty of these structures that seem to be beyond the works of man. And in the foreground the magnificent Sphinx which spells eternity itself. It was a gorgeous morning. Not too hot. And the sky was blue as blue. Ed [Terrace] was a wonderful guide once we could shake the [illegible] who was ever at our heels. Between the paws of the Sphinx we saw where Tutmosis had slept and erected a monument which describes his dream. In it he was told to excavate and he would find the forelegs and paws of the monument. And he did! The pyramid temple of Chephren is a wonder of masonry construction: the size and cutting of the blocks staggers the imagination.

Then we relaxed at the refreshment house and drank lemonade. But not before I became the total tourist and rode round on a camel and had my picture taken to prove that I had been here! The others can be blasé about the whole experience. But not I.

The only flaw is that you aren't here to see all this with me and show me around. And of course it would be great if P&E&B were in the caravan too. I think of you all the time.

GLENVEAGH CASTLE, DONEGAL

22 JULY 1968

Dear Heart,

This was the best idea—to pause here and rest up for the weekend before the last stand of the voyage on the homebound plane on Friday next.[229] I may get to Boston before this letter, I realize, but I have to write it anyway. I certainly owe you another and there is so much to say.

I sleep and read, swim and walk. And of course I eat the most delicious food and drink my share. The one flaw in this cocoon is that you are not with me. For I think except Cairo you would have enjoyed it most of all the places I have unpacked my bags. I'm in a room in the lesser tower: all pink and purple and black Victorian lacquer with mother-of-pearl, a pile of new books by the bed, roses here and roses there. Elgie is below me and was the only inmate when I came. But now there are four more: Two Dutch ladies, a Countess Linden van something and a Mrs. Loudon whose husband used to run Royal Dutch Shell and knows the Tafts and other Bostonians as the Loudons used to live there . . .

Fourteen for dinner last night with black tie. I never met half the guests, but had a perfectly good time with those I did. Today in the rain we picnicked at the stalking lodge. I walked all the way to and from—two and three quarters miles each, with the lovely golden retrievers—three of them—bounding ahead of me. Gorgeous picnic lunch—curried chicken.

---

229. Much as he had with Peggy Guggenheim in Venice, Rathbone made a habit of visiting Henry McIlhenny at Glenveagh, his Victorian castle in Donegal, Ireland, during Rathbone's summer tours of Europe.

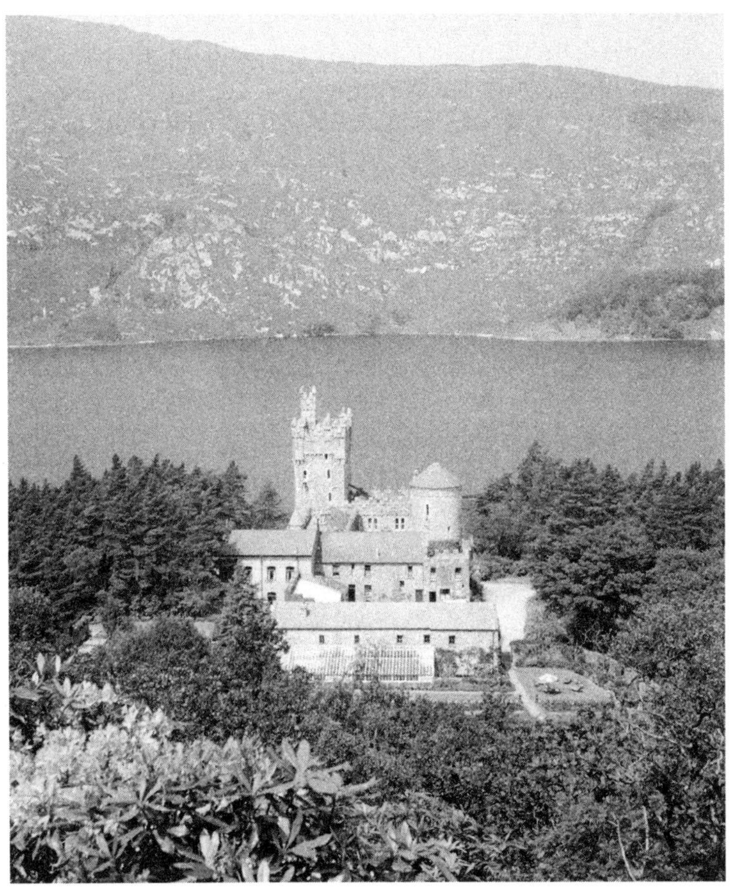

Glenvaegh Castle in Donegal, Ireland in the 1960s.

Remember to put a little apricot jam in the curry sauce! Then raspberries of all shades. On the return the Klenks and I swam from the beach, practically nude. And yesterday I swam from the dock and felt incredibly strong and healthy. Elgie wears a copper bracelet against arthritis and rheumatism. I'm getting you one in London.

Edinburgh charmed me utterly. Its neat stone buildings,

rational order, its cleanliness, its beautiful park sweeping
down then up to that spine of grand old castles, spires and
whatnot, its polished crimson and white busses, cheerful
good-looking people, its solid plainness after all the frippery
of continental cities. You feel somehow secure amongst a
wonderfully capable, disciplined and intelligent people. But
God knows there is nothing to do after 10 pm. The National
Gallery is a dream. Rich, but not big, bright and clean. The
director was most kind and would have taken me home to
lunch if I had let him.

Harry Polwarth was going out of town when I arrived. But
the second night he drove me down to his ancestral acres,
Harden Hawick (pronounced Hoik) about one and a half
hours from Edinburgh. The plain old border country house
is packed with portraits and memorabilia including a family
tree made out by Sir Walter Scott, the Bible of his first titled
ancestor of Jacobean times. I was immersed in Scottish border
lore. Harry has grayed and looks older than I do, though he
is only fifty-two. His nice son, Andrew was with him, though
Carol alas was in England with the girls. In the morning
at 8:15 I took a first class plush and very clean carriage to
Edinburgh—one and a half hours and fell happily to sleep
after devouring the *Times* which Andrew had nipped out of
the car and bought for me while pausing at a traffic light.
Quelle politesse!

I think Scotland would make a lovely little trip someday.

HOTEL PORTA ROSSA, FIRENZE
15 JULY 1969

Darling Rett,

Here I am in your old home town[230] and loving every minute of it and wishing so much you were with me to savor all the old sights and tread the old stones.

No Billy, but at least a letter at last. Too bad, for he missed a delightful tour with the best companions one could find. Of course it was very art historical and mildly alcoholic too as we always drank deep of the local wine and sucked on a two-liter bottle of slivovitz in the car—very good fuel for long passages on the highway. John [Goelet] did all the driving in his Mercedes, and wonderfully well. He is most adept at biting the nails on one hand and driving with the other.

After Salzburg, St. Florian, Kloster Neuburg and Heiligen Kranz we had a day and a half in Wien where we spent a long evening with Hofstatter and looked at everything in his flat. We were also cheated out of a visit to the Kunsthistorisches Museum as the thing closes at 3 pm. Then we drove south through the very beautiful countries of Styria and Carinthia, stopping the night at Seckau in a charming eighteenth century inn where our bedroom ceiling was decorated with Pyramus and Thisbe in high stucco relief. We found wonderful things in the neighboring huge monastery. We stopped at Friesach and Gurk and then over the pass into Friuli and to Udine for the night. Afro[231] unfortunately in hospital, so we missed him.

---

230. After leaving Cairo in 1919, Rettles' father bought an olive farm outside of Florence.

231. Afro Basaldella (1912–1976) was an Italian artist and friend of long acquaintance.

A lively night with [Bruno] Lorenzellis who filled us with good food and wine and feasted our eyes with their collection and poured out many compliments about you and the girls.

In Genoa we made our rendezvous with John Shearman[232] on the dot and thus commenced the greatest of all adventures—negotiations for the Raphael (CONFIDENTIALLY) which ended in success. J[ohn] S[hearman] was entirely sure of it and thoroughly captivated. That evening after dining with old Ildebrando [Bossi][233] . . . at his villa at Recco on the Riviera we closed the deal with me as spokesman in my best French (!) and John following up with discussion of the financial details—and with great heart. Of course I can hardly believe it. Then Sunday our host wanted us all to come back to Recco for lunch and so we did after which John departed and Hanns [Swarzenski] and I spent the afternoon sunbathing and I swam and swam again from the rocks.

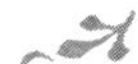

232. John Shearman (1931–2003) was an English art historian considered a leading expert in the work of Raphael. He was invited to authenticate a painting attributed to Raphael that Rathbone was considering for the MFA. The story of the "Portrait of a Young Girl" is thoroughly covered in *The Boston Raphael*, Belinda Rathbone, Boston: Godine, 2014.

233. Ildebrando Bossi was a Genoese dealer who sold the painting attributed to Raphael to the MFA and later died in prison on charges of illegal export.

From the Journal of the Aegean Cruise, August 7 - 21, 1973[234]

7 AUGUST

Sailed from Piraeus at 12:10 after much scrambled photography on the *Astral* and the *Goose* a toast to the voyage with all the crew and traditional libation to Poseidon over the side. Constantine and his photographer on hand. No crisis over breadcrumbs as on our last cruise when the cook refused to sail without!

15 AUGUST

Parga charmed us from the first glimpse, rising up from the neat little bay against majestic mountains. We were able to tie up at end of long pier and to our surprise the *Astral* came alongside. Very matey. Our splendid boats caused great stir and curiosity. A crowd gathered and we went ashore, heading straight for the new but already famous shirt shop whose sign, Pargamour, was even too conspicuous. Shop shut for Assumption. Wandered up and up with Emmy and Joe to remains of the Castro. Most picturesque harbor with tiny islands and a tiny chapel. After dinner on board we gathered (in) a

---

234. This was Rathbone's fifth Aegean cruise as the guest of Henry McIlhenny with a party of regulars, beginning in 1962. On board the *Astral* and the *Silver Goose* were Patricia Clark, Emlen and Gloria Etting, Henry McIlhenny, Joseph and Emily Rauh Pulitzer, Kate Davis Quesada, Perry and Rettles Rathbone.

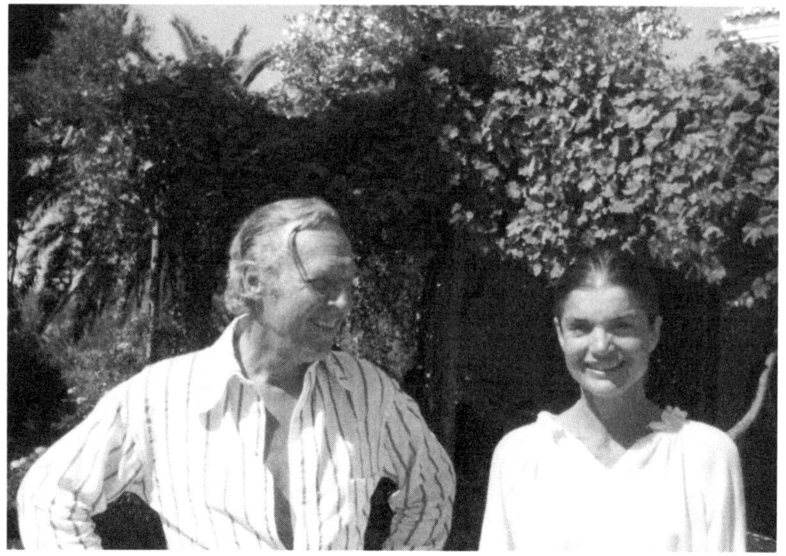

Rathbone anchors at the Greek island of Skorpios for a visit
with Jackie Onassis in August 1973.

dancing square on the waterfront which was crammed with citizens young and old. Six man bouzouki band provided music
and the smallest children frolicked and danced as much as the
elders.

Now we were once again near Skorpios and spurred by Rettles'
urging I simply asked the captain to call the Onassis on our
radio-telephone and say that I was nearby on the *Silver Goose*. It
takes time to make contact thus, but within an hour and a half
as I was cocktailing with the others on *Astral*, message came
that Mr. O. was on the phone for me. Having first established
that I was the same Perry Rathbone who was director of the
Boston Museum, he expressed regret that he would have to be
in Athens the next day but that his wife would be delighted
to have us all for lunch. This she would confirm following

morning at 9:30. The electrifying effect of this message on my fellow passengers was laughed off with a few jokes. And soon the discussion turned to appropriate attire for the occasion. Next morning promptly at 9:30 a speed boat appeared leaving the captain of the *Christina* asking for Mr. Rathbone. "Mrs. Onassis expects all of you for lunch. Please come to Skorpios at 12:30."

Coiffed and groomed and still a bit awed by our good luck and what awaited us, we sailed into the little harbor alongside the *Christina* where the captain greeted us and asked us our pleasure: a swim? A tour of the island? A couple of little cars appeared and in two waves we toured the island, more ravishing at close range. At many places along the winding little roads were banks of flowers, zinnias such as I had never seen, plumbago, impatiens, petunias by the thousands and surprisingly even hydrangea, and beautiful plantings of trees everywhere.

The captain had told us that lunch would be at the "pink house." Hardly had the second group returned to the dock, i.e. myself, Rettles, and Pat, when Jackie appeared. Mrs. O. looked enchanting and as always, original. Tall and dressed in soft white cotton tunic with billowing sleeves and long pants, her hair tied back severely in a ponytail, her face accented by immense round sunglasses. She greeted me in her quiet way but with genuine warmth and we strolled up to the waiting jeeps and Jackie drove us up to the pink house, we still hardly believing that we were actually in the midst of this paradise, guests of one of the most famous women alive and I think, probably the most charming. The pink house gave me the impression of being buried in flowers. We walked along a path bordered with jasmine and soon found ourselves in the enchanting loggia roofed with rustic branches and vines. Just off the loggia a big V-shaped flower bed overflowing with lavender petunias in bright sunshine. Principal feature of the loggia were four low wicker chairs, each filled invitingly with a big cushion covered with India print. Two guests quietly blended themselves into our group after Jackie's introduction. One was a handsome young Frenchman, Thierry de Beaucé, a member of the foreign office soon to leave for Peking and Hanoi to reestablish French diplomatic and trade relations; the other the Contessa Brandolini, the good-looking blonde Venetian wife of Guido B. whose family I know. I talked with Mrs. O. about the garden and the planting of the island. She gave Ari full credit and emphasized his devotion to the whole plantation.

After drinks twice around lunch was served buffet style in the adjacent big and airy room: Russian salad with lobster, Beef Wellington, pasticcio, cold red wine. We sat around informally in the loggia, some at a long table, others in the big chairs and I continued my conversation with Jackie. Stimulated by some incident in my career that I related, she was rather insistent that I should write my memoirs. There is something almost unreal about Jackie's face. It's as square as a box and her eyes are unbelievably wideset and unbelievably big and lustrous. All this is accentuated without her usual frame of hair and made exotic by the immense discs of her glasses frames—like the eyes of a mantis. Even without her looks, she would be a fascinating woman. In spite of her sophistication she retains an ingenuous manner, speaking slowly and quietly. And she really listens so that you feel you engage her entire attention. After the delicious lunch served by a French major domo and Greek waiter with the most expansive smile yet seen, Jackie led us away from the guest pink house up the slope to the Onassis house, explaining that the house was not really Ari's home. His home is the yacht, the *Christina*. He sleeps in the house, Jackie explained, but he is very apt to go down to the *Christina* to shave in the morning! She always referred to him as "Ari."

JAPAN

Kyoto is an education in itself. It's a delight moreover, even in the rain and it has rained without cease for thirty-six hours. In Kyoto you are hand in glove with the ancient past at every turn. And you feel that here there has been a more consistent and serious cultivation of beauty for its own sake than anywhere in the world. Though corrupted by modern times, by industrial Japan, the sense of beauty is alive in all the traditional locations of the city. In gardens, temples, palaces it is alive in whatever corner of the city nature is cultivated. The Japanese infatuation with nature one never ceases to marvel at. It takes so many shapes: the branch of a budding tree in a meiping vase in a shop window, the plantings of willows and flowering trees on the banks of the river, the streams of water and waterfalls, the exquisite pruning of the gingko trees. Nature is constantly in the eye and on the mind of the Japanese.

This is my fourth visit[1] yet I feel I have just begun to know Kyoto. One reason is that I have had to explore and find my way about on my own. I've walked through the Gion quarter for the first time. Here old Kyoto remains almost intact, streets of

---

1. Rathbone's fourth visit to Japan was on the occasion of an Andrew Wyeth exhibition he organized, sponsored by the Japanese newspaper the *Nihon Keizai Shimbun* in Tokyo. This was the direct result of a Wyeth retrospective at the MFA that Rathbone organized for the centennial, which was an enormous popular success.

small-scale houses, red lanterns at the doors, the names of the Geisha inhabitants on wood panels fixed by the entrance. Sadly telephone and electricity poles and overhead wires disturb the antique harmony of the scene. The quarter is filled with antique shops and shopping is an irresistible pastime in Kyoto. And it can be as expensive for antiques as it is cheap for modern objects—toys, novelties, usable things—in the ancient craft tradition where perfect taste and good workmanship go hand in hand. For one like me, temptations abound and only natural caution and circumspection about spending and the ever present disapproval of my sensible Rettles deters me from satisfying passing whims and age-old desires. Sir John Figgess, Christie's man in Tokyo, gave me the name of Yamagi in this quarter. He received me most charmingly and I whiled away an hour as he brought out the best of his potteries, early ones—Seto, Shino. I admired extravagantly a black glazed husky Seto tea bowl. Asking if I liked Japanese tea, in a moment it was brought back with the beautiful green brew lying in its bottom. I drank it formally in three noisy swallows to Mr. Yamagi's delight.

Figgess has extolled the virtues of Gombei's soba shop nearby and when Yamagi invited me to lunch I eagerly recommended Gombei. There we lunched without shoes on the best soba yet, and a bottle of beer.

I'm in need of a box of drawers for my new writing table at the New York flat.[2] From an undistinguished modern one in a craft shop in Kawaramachi street my taste and ambition escalated alarmingly until I found myself buying a beautiful

---

2. Following his retirement from the MFA in 1972, Rathbone became director of Christie's New York office in 1973, one of the perks of which was a two-bedroom apartment at 40 East Seventy-Eighth Street. With the opening of their New York auction rooms on Park Avenue, he continued as museums liaison for Christie's until retiring in 1986.

antique Korean piece inlaid with mother of pearl and dating back to the Yi Dynasty, a sixteenth-century piece. Price about $630.00 instead of $30.00 for a modern Japanese one. A big leap and extravagance but I justify it by reason of my Keizai earnings and my pennywise economies such as washing my socks and breakfasting on Nescafé, taking busses and streetcars. Korean pieces, I learn, are rare and always expensive. Yamagi's young assistant assures me the price is not high.

Lived through the second heaviest rainfall since the Meiji Dynasty began.

Bussed to Osaka, the bus jammed with Japanese. No room for my knees and my head hit the ceiling when I stood up. Had to run like fury through the vast and forbidding Osaka airport to catch my little plane to Takamatsu.

Lovely mountainous distance greets you at Tak airport. Noguchi's[3] assistant, Ishima, met me and drove me through the uglified fringes of Tak till we came to a veritable stone lantern land—hundreds on every side and being granite and rock yards and ugly corrugated sheds. At the end of the road is Noguchi's transplanted samurai house.

This lovely abode was built in the eighteenth century in the region of Takamoto and was about to fall victim to modern road building. An intelligent local supervisor of antiquities saw its possibilities. It suited Noguchi's needs, so he was happy to settle in it. In fact he was overjoyed because the place is his tax-free. The locale is not exactly ideal. The surrounding stone-cutting industry is not very pretty. The landscape is dotted with corrugated iron shelters. One is Noguchi's built to construct his big abstraction for N.Y. State U at Purchase, N.Y.

---

3. Rathbone had tendered an invitation to visit Isamu Noguchi's home and studio in Takamoto.

The house is good outside and in, the latter is fully the serene geometry of the characteristic Japanese interior and the contrasts of very dark and very light. Dark heavy beams, straw tatami, featherweight shoji in white paper. Further geometry is provided by Noguchi's lamps and lanterns made of paper and bamboo and known throughout the world. The newest are made without bamboo ribs, simply a geometric light wire frame.

A bit taken aback by N.'s appearance when he finally came on stage minutes after my arrival. He has stepped into old manhood: bald pate, gray fringe of hair, lined face, the state accentuated by his halting, painful gait brought on by a muscular spasm. This he sought constantly and unsuccessfully to relieve during my stay. He wore a dark gray kimono which is very becoming to him and dignified. But his distinguished appearance and his fame have little effect upon his disposition. I did not want to believe it from previous meetings, but this man is querulous, envious, and a malcontent. Most artists are self-centered and often jealous of their rivals. Noguchi seems to be a case of incurable discontent. No generous thought of anybody. Especially peeved because Tokyo's Chase Bank project was not accepted. He said he knows no reason. Perhaps he did too much, he mused. An old habit of mind. When I first met him in St. Louis twenty-five years ago, he accused me of buying no modern art except from Curt Valentin. Of all the sculptors I have known—Moore, Marini, Calder, Milles, Lipchitz, Marcks—Noguchi is the only one who lacks basic kindliness. He received me with little more than a perfunctory greeting. I am the only one who has invited himself to his abode, he said. Not exactly surprising.

Noguchi's maid and cook showed me to my room where I was to sleep on tatami. Meanwhile a bath was offered and I eagerly accepted. The old samurai house has a fine new bathroom. An immense circular wooden tub, clear white stock filling up with steaming water. It stands on a floor of loose cobbles amongst which are placed three or four log sections which provide a path to the tub. There I steeped myself for a quarter of an hour, water to my chin, legs folded in front of me. Surely this is closest to returning to the womb of any experience on earth.

Dinner guests were frequent visitors to the Noguchi house. One was the self-effacing Isami, perfect as Noguchi's assistant. Another was the simpatico Yamamoto, a giant Japanese—my height—who is director of the Prefectural architecture office. A man of great modernity and remarkable talent. Limited English. Ready laugh. Understands artists. He himself as an architect is an artist like [William] Bernoudy. Rare bird. I liked him instinctively and especially. The other guest was a broadcaster. The nice cook-waitress joined us at the almost floor-level table. Delicious Japanese meal with grilled seabass as feature.

Contrary to expectation N. seemed to wish me to meet [Masayuki] Nagare[4] who lives on the other side of the mountain and from all accounts a mountain is not too much to stand between them. Yamamoto arranged to put the governor's (of the Prefecture) car at my disposal and in the morning I drove off with Yamamoto from the Prefectural building at Takamatsu to see the new Seto Folk Culture of the Inland Sea Museum ten kilometers out of town. Young girl interpreter accompanied us—too shy to utter a word of English. Good building, one of the best small museums I know and a spectacular site, high above Inland Sea. Lunch at a neighboring popular restaurant. Then along a winding coastal road to see Nagare in his new house,

---

4. Masayuki Nagare (1923–2018) was a modernist Japanese sculptor whose work in stone derives from traditional martial arts.

a kind of red brick stronghold on the far side of the peninsula, out of sight of every sign of industry and commanding a superlative view of the sea, distant coastline, and islands.

Nagare was smiling and informal and happy to show me over his domain with the speechless interpreter (Yamamoto had a meeting to attend) inside and out. Architect was his sculpture assistant and is decidedly amateur-ish, but not without charm. And N. has charm too as Noguchi has not. Also a good sense of humor. When I commented that Madame Butterfly also came from Nagasaki, he said, "Madame Butterfly was my mother!" His English is quite good. But he persistently refused to allow me to photograph him, saying "I'm only a country boy!" Which to me was no reason. But I suspect he didn't want to be photographed in his work clothes. He was dressed in plaid shirt, blue jeans and a little cotton work cap. His other photo portraits are rather ennobling, not exactly candid. He's more like the sculptural fraternity I've known. That is, openhearted and retaining some of the innocence or simplicity of a child as compared with Noguchi's brittle self-centeredness. He produced whiskey highballs twice. A bit of swagger here, perhaps. Anyway he's obviously rich with his big commissions—Bank of America, Tokyo World Trade Center—for example—things that incite Noguchi's jealousy.

He's a master of the rough and smooth and the samurai sword in his background is very often present. Nagare preceded Noguchi to Takamatsu presumably to take advantage of the stone lantern cutters concentrated there.

I think Noguchi a bit nervous about the need to entertain me and seemed relieved that I'd take my departure in spite of transit strike which gripped Japan. Actually got to airport one hour ahead of time!

*　*　*

Tokyo again and the New Otani. Wyeth show well on the track. Big crowds—over three thousand on Saturday and Sunday—big catalog sale—one to every five visitors. As I predicted, though A. W. is virtually unknown, he has the strong appeal for the Japanese. All *Shimbun* and museum people very pleased. Even the undemonstrative [Jiro] Enjoji.[5] Visitors look long and hard at the paintings, very quiet and studious. Favorite postcard is young bull, Betsy (Maga's Daughter) is second.

Saturday morning Enjoji's car fetched me from the Otani to his office. This was the day of the pay-off. Myata Ohara as interpreter and Enjoji appeared. After the customary tea and smiles of satisfaction were exchanged some office boys brought the yen, P.T.R.'s yen. Piles of it in neat packets of ten thousand notes bound with tape. A very precise accounting was made: The $5,000 down payment which I had left with the *Shimbun* at interest (minus 15% tax) plus the $10,000 in yen representing the balance. Then Enjoji presented me with a gift elaborately boxed and wrapped, a red lacquer plate with a golden heron flying in the middle; not my taste at all. But feigned delight. Handshakes and farewells. Then straight to the Bank of Tokyo on foot (the bundled yen in a shopping bag) with Miyata and Ohara and there opened a yen account at 7.5%. A most accommodating bank staffer assisted me. Matter was complicated by need to make payments to the Kyoto shopkeepers for the Korean box of drawers and the Edo bamboo lamp. Then we parted and as I walked alone through the streets of Tokyo I felt absolutely euphoric: accomplishment, security, a little of myself planted in a city I love. And a source to be tapped on future visits.

---

5. Jiro Enjoji was managing director of the *Nihon Keizai Shimbun*, the newspaper sponsors of the Andrew Wyeth exhibition.

AFTERWORD

MY FATHER RETURNED to Japan in 1974 to oversee the closing of the Andrew Wyeth exhibition, and again in 1985 on various business projects. He had retired from the MFA in 1972 and in 1973 accepted an offer from Christie's to head their New York office. At the time, Christie's occupied the second floor of the Rhinelander mansion on the corner of Madison Avenue and 72nd Street. When the firm opened their New York saleroom in the Delmonico Hotel on Park Avenue in 1977, they retained my father in a full-time position as Museums Liaison which he enjoyed until his retirement in 1986.

By the early 1970s his journal writing had come to an end, and he was engaged with another kind of personal record keeping. The Archives of American Art dispatched Paul Cummings to conduct a sixteen-hour interview with him over several months from 1975–1976. The Columbia University Center for Oral History did much the same in 1981–1982, with interviewer Raymond Daum. It was an opportunity to remember and to reflect on his museum years, which he did with remarkable clarity and personal insight, to the rapt attention of his interlocutors. These interviews left us with a treasure as valuable, if not quite as spontaneous, as the journals he wrote during the height of his career.

ILLUSTRATIONS

PAGE 165 Glenvaegh Castle, Ireland. Photograph by Perry T. Rathbone. *Copyright © Perry T. Rathbone.*

PAGE 170 Rathbone and Jackie Onassis, Greece. Photographer unknown. *Courtesy of the Rathbone family.*

ACKNOWLEDGEMENTS

OUT OF a sense of shared interest in family history, I began to transcribe my father's journals with the enthusiastic help of my niece Sarah Rathbone in 2006. What emerged from these handwritten pages became an invaluable resource in the writing of my 2014 book about my father, *The Boston Raphael.* These ten years later, I was encouraged to publish the journals to stand alone. I am grateful to my editor Joshua Bodwell for seeing the value in the project and for seeing it through to publication, and also to Celia Johnson for her sensitive edit. Enormous thanks also go to my brother, Peter, and sister, Eliza, for consenting to the publication but far beyond that, for actively collaborating in the entry selections. I believe the result is a better book than it would have been without their input, for though we all lived those years with our father, we lived and saw them differently, as siblings do, and it is the combination of our eyes on the content that makes the best of its many sides.

A NOTE ON THE TYPE

In the Company of Art has been set in Janson. Our text face owes it's revival to Chauncey H. Griffith of Merganthaler Linotype, 1937. It's been discovered that this type is originally the work of Nicholas Kis (1650-1702), a Hungarian, who most probably learned his trade from the master Dutch type founder Dirk Hoskens. Janson is held in high regard for being both readable and handsome.

Design & Composition by Brooke Koven

w. 3 dances + a reception.

Today came an invitation from the President + Mrs. Kennedy to Dine at the White House Nov. 13. We have accepted.

24 Oct.

Cleaning of Degas' 'Carriage at the races' is completed. This small masterwork is now a pearl. From under an old veil of discolored varnish + dirt emerges a landscape w. figures bathed in clean air, a sky dotted w. tiny puffs of vapor, a vast sweep of field of a tender indescribable green. The sunshine described is soft, luminescent. This is surely one of the triumphs of 'plein airism' without reliance on the Impressionist technique of broken color. Bought for $30,000 in 1926 by the Museum, it is surely worth $230,000 today. Work has begun on cleaning the 'Jockeys', another tiny jewel of the coll. acquired in 1903 for $9000. The ... severely crackled sky has been overpainted w. a deep creamy color wh. J. Finlayson is now removing to reveal a sky of pinkish-purplish tint which has form + air.

Odyssia Skouras of Rome, a young + pretty art dealer + friend of the Berninis called on me. To Gios. Castano w. Harris to look at 2 childe Hassams — a w.c. + an oil. He gave me each a page of gouaches of Neapolitan scenes of the 1840's.

28. Rettles to Brooks to fetch Peter on our ...